It is easy to go down into hell; night and day, the gates of dark death stand wide to climb back again, to retrace ones steps to the upper air—there's the rub, the task ... *Virgil, from Aeneid*

1968 – Into the Abyss

BY

Riley St. James

www.rileystjames.com

Copyright © 2012

All rights reserved. No part of this book may be reproduced in any form or by any electronic or mechanical means, including information storage and retrieval systems, without written permission from the authors, except in the case of a reviewer, who may quote brief passages embodied in critical articles or in a review.

Foreword

Warfare on a Skewer?

On May 14, 1845, with a seasonal wet monsoon building to pound the Indochinese coast, an American war party of U.S. sailors and Marines stormed the shores of Danang, South Vietnam…Wait…is there a typo here? No, no typo here. The first clash between the United States and Vietnam (then Turon, Cochin China) occurred in May of 1845 and lasted for twelve days, as officially recorded by U.S. Navy logs.

On May 10 the mighty American frigate USS Constitution, nicknamed "Old Ironsides," under command of Captain John Percival, dropped anchor in the bay that bordered what is known today as Danang, Vietnam. (The anchor location was near what would become known as Monkey Mountain to Americans during the modern Vietnam War.) Percival's initial mission was peaceful — to bury a musician, named Paul Cooke, who had recently died aboard the ship that was on a worldwide voyage, far from home of Charleston, North Carolina.

Following a cordial welcome by Danang's authorities — termed "Mandarins" by the Americans — the arrangements were made to lay Cooke to rest in an attractive plot within a native burial ground nestled at the foot of a mountain. On the following morning all went as planned. The peaceful ceremony was completed in proper fashion and was promptly followed by Percival and his crew returning to the ship.

On the fourth day of their anchorage, however, the serene atmosphere dramatically changed. While the ship was being upgraded and watered to prepare for sea, Captain Percival received an alerting message from a villager that a French Missionary, Bishop Domenique Lefevre, was imprisoned by the Danang Mandarins; and the bishop had already been tried and sentenced to death. Crumpling the message with a rigid clench, Percival stiffened and turned toward the city with a determined stare. He hastily decided he would carry out a humanitarian deed and rescue the Bishop from these "nearly barbarous natives," as he called them, without regard as to why the Bishop's fate had been so dastardly sealed. (Captain Percival was known on the high seas for his impetuous and headstrong nature—nicknamed "Mad Jack" by his naval peers.)

For the next six days, Percival attempted everything within his power to free the Bishop. He first directed a threatening war party consisting of sailors and half of the ship's regular squad of sixty Marines to storm into the city to intimidate the mandarins and demand the immediate release of the Bishop. (What's incredible about this recorded incident, is that the first 3,500 combat designated troops of the modern Vietnam conflict landed on these very same shores in 1965—and they were also Marines.)

When Percival's boisterous tactic failed to rile the Mandarins, or produce any clue as to the Bishop's whereabouts, or further gather any evidence that the Bishop actually existed, the agitated Marines seized three defenseless Mandarins as hostages and exited the city. And for extra measure, when the sailors reached the shoreline, they commandeered three dilapidated Chinese junkets, anchoring them in the bay close to the *Constitution*. Meanwhile, the Mandarins continued to mount no resistance. They simply stood on the beach, shrugged and watched the rowdy Americans in confused silence.

As the days passed, Captain Percival would sporadically compound his huffing and puffing shenanigans by standing on the battery deck and ordering a few of the 24-pounder long-guns to fire toward one of the forts located at the edge of the city. Meant only as another reckless warning, Percival would ensure the cannons were trained to have the iron projectiles purposely fall short.

Nevertheless, Cochin Emperor, Thieu Tri, growing impatient and now openly irritated, wouldn't budge under any of Percival's aggressive pressure. He sent word to the anxious captain that absolutely nothing would be accomplished until the Americans ceased their hostile incursion so that talks could begin. (At this point, there were more conflicting reports on whether any Bishop was even being held on the island.)

Finally, on May 24, after days of wrangling and a few isolated incidents of "pushing and shoving" on land, yet neither group suffering casualties, Percival decided that his animated bluffing had failed. Therefore, he submitted to the Emperor's demands and released the junkets and hostages to demonstrate his "good will."

A strained, but confident Captain Percival retreated to his cabin while fully expecting that the liberated Bishop would soon appear, board the frigate, and the crew could weigh anchor and proudly commence with the remainder of their voyage. Yet Percival's wait proved fruitless while the crew battled a ferocious wind-swept downpour that pelted the area, adding to his exasperation. Finally, Percival dispatched a message of final warning to the emperor: *If the ship sailed without the Bishop he would report this matter to the French authorities when he arrived at Canton, China, and surely they would return to seek the Bishop and inflict revengeful justice on the Mandarins!*

However, the only activity that Emperor Thieu Tri was involved in was further flaunting his defiance by fortifying Danang's beachhead, and the surrounding fields in plain view of the frigate, which enabled the frustrated captain to clearly observe their preparations. Moreover, the Mandarins had summoned a few Chinese ships from Hue, the Cochin capital. While those armed ships slowly passed the frigate as they entered the bay, Percival concluded that he might have taken on more than he could handle and gave his executive officers orders to prepare for sea.

On May 26, 1845, the outraged Percival weighed anchor for Tunisia to continue his intended voyage. Fully underway toward the open sea, he ordered a volley of long-gun bursts toward a vulnerable cluster of hamlets located at the outskirts of the city, inflicting little if any damage. Ironically, for all his bluster and trouble, Percival hadn't even laid eyes on the Bishop, much more liberate him. Everything had virtually been left the same as they were when the *Constitution* arrived sixteen days before—except perhaps, precipitating some tense relations between Washington and China, even though President James Polk apparently had no direct bearing on Percival's rash actions while anchored at Danang.

As the Indochinese coastline faded from view, one of Percival's officers, Fifth Lieutenant John B. Dale, wrote in his journal: "...it seems, I must say, to have shown a sad want of 'sound discretion,' in commencing an affair of this kind, without carrying it through to a successful conclusion."

****

Incredibly, Lieutenant Dale hardly knew then how accurate and prophetic his words would loom over a century later.

America Storms Ashore: In March 1965 the first American combat troops stormed ashore — with 3,500 Marines landing on that same Danang beach. To support America's combat escalation nearly 20,000 men per month were being drafted for active duty. And by June 74,000 Americans were deployed in Vietnam. In October 1965 the first major ground battle involving American troops occurred at Plei Me, in the Ia Drang Valley. Both sides suffered heavy losses. By the end of 1965, the Vietnam campaign was at a new phase, officially dubbed "Counteroffensive." U.S. military strength was 200,000 and climbing. By the end of 1967, U.S. troop deployment had reached a staggering 475,000. Regardless of the increasing political strife that besieged Washington in late 1968, troop strength was still rising, reaching 510,000. Deaths in that year alone totaled 16,589, not including the wounded and missing; nearly 39,000 had died to date.

In 1969 the Nixon Doctrine, intended to end the war with honor, was put into effect. Nevertheless, by spring, military strength had peaked at 543,000. But gradually the complexion of the country began to change. The reduction strategy of U.S. military was in place and 25,000 troops were withdrawn by September. This demonstrated the "Vietnamization" phase had been set in motion — South Vietnam would take over the warfare, while the Americans steadily pulled out and went home.

The final major ground battle involving U.S. military occurred in

October 1971. Throughout that year U.S. strength was continually reduced and those units that remained were converted to a defensive status. By the end of the year there were less than 200,000 troops in Vietnam, the lowest level in six years. The troop withdrawal continued while the peace process including a total cease-fire was being negotiated in Paris. An agreement—the Treaty of Paris—was finally achieved and formally signed in January 1973 by all parties. (South Vietnam remained reluctant, but signed.)

America exits: In April 1975 the North Vietnamese forces raged into the South and annihilated all major defenses. Whatever Americans remained—military and civilian—were safely evacuated from Saigon. The day after that city was taken over by the North, it was renamed Ho Chi Minh City, in tribute to the late leader who thirty years before had officially implored President Harry Truman to allow him to accomplish the same goal of reunifying the country—only peacefully.

Ho Chi Minh seemed to know then that reunification was inevitable, regardless of the human sacrifices and time that the effort would require. The major difference then was that Minh assured Truman that if Vietnam were allowed to proceed independently, Minh's regime would hold national elections, which would unify the North and South under one elected government. One can only wonder whether Minh's proposal would have occurred had Truman granted him the opportunity. But certainly America might have been spared warfare.

Aftermath: Although fourteen countries participated in the modern Vietnam conflict, it is widely believed that Americans suffered the severest consequences: More than 58,000 Americans died (eight women), or are MIA's (missing in action); and over 300,000 wounded. This does not include an obscure but significant number of U.S civilians that had served in a humanitarian role—such as nurses—that remain unaccounted for. The actual dollars spent reached well over a hundred fifty billion. And calling the many years of American combat in Vietnam a "War" can only be done so idiomatically, because no U.S. administration that was involved in the decades-long military struggle ever officially declared War on Vietnam. And regardless of the American war process that prevailed for three decades, Vietnam still became unified under one government. In 1976 North and South officially became one, the Socialist Republic of Vietnam.

Indeed, as the USS Constitution sailed away from Danang on May 26, 1845, Lieutenant Dale's words, "...it seems, I must say, to have shown a sad want of 'sound discretion,' in commencing an affair of this kind, without carrying it through to a successful conclusion," had evidently lain ignored, except by the country for which they were intended.

Riley St. James

Prologue

The Elite Tunnel Rats

Throughout any warfare in history you will find countless heroes and seemingly exceptional military units of men encrusted with a loyal and indomitable shell to battle for their country well beyond of what is asked or required; some units are often celebrated and easily recognizable, others are not. This is a story of one of those distinctive squads that is *not*: a small band of fearless fighters who volunteered to carve out their piece of bloodstained history during the height of the Viet Nam Conflict, named the "offensive phase," when U.S. troop strength was reaching 500,000. Although tunnel discovery came to light in the spring of 1967, this unit was one of the first to be officially called "Tunnel Rats" after their record of heroic war feats began to emerge through the leafy canopy of the steamy Southeast Asian jungles.

Adapted from the actual war annals of former *Rat* leader and Special Forces soldier, Staff Sergeant, Thomas E. Wergen—*Bronze Star Medal* and *Combat Infantryman Badge* recipient—this book centers on his elite unit of American mavericks who would blindly descend into the dank darkness to meander, creep, seek out and encounter the enemy where even the most courageous were unwilling to venture—the dreaded and combat-terrifying jungle tunnels built by the North Vietnamese forces. These forces consisted of both the North's regular army and the South's insurgent *Viet Cong*, who were armed northern sympathizers technically recognized by Ho Chi Minh; *Cong* contemptuously meant "commies" to the Saigon regime. (The American military nicknamed them "Charlie.")

During the lengthy and horrific six years when America was actually caught up in intense ground combat operations, from the first vicious Viet Cong attack at the Ia Drang Valley to the final major ground battle at Thua Thien Province in 1971, there were many daring soldiers who would bravely volunteer (never ordered) to explore and challenge the harrowing risks of destroying (denying) the tunnels when discovered.

Yet perhaps Wergen's small outfit stands out as the most legendary and effective group of tunnel rats to ever come together. With adrenaline running high and unrelenting allegiance to watching each other's backs, they thrived on encountering, searching and denying hundreds of tunnels, the more complex and dangerous the better. This became their main warfare responsibility. They were the professionals and the rookie-trainers of their time — no claustrophobia or panic allowed — only patience, eyes, ears, weapon and sheer guts. (No *Rat* candidate would be allowed to join Wergen's squad unless all current *Rats* steadfastly agreed. There was absolutely no tolerance for a "weak link" to bring down the team while entangled with deadly perils within their *underground abyss*.)

As though he were rolled right out of "Central Casting" for a commando war epic, Wergen had it all: prime manhood, handsome, intelligent, courageously rugged with a confident and calm leadership aura, and a professional trained background in chemicals and demolition. He was just what the Army needed, and found.

Soon after Wergen began his tour, he volunteered to lead the Rats when they were only informally acknowledged and regarded as a "blue collar" group of the special combat squads. Beginning as ragtag and loosely organized with no particular training or strategy, the *Rats* were afforded no extraordinary recognition, if any formal tribute at all.

They wore no fancy uniforms or decorative berets. They gained no benefit from any self-serving ballad, and sported virtually no famed reputation similar to those of the other corps of the Special Forces. They simply trudged through and war-worked the enemy-peppered jungles whenever summoned. But their unpretentious status would gradually grow bolder as the war escalated and the demand increased for the efficient and devastating skills this extraordinary team of Tunnel Rats employed to challenge the treacherous North Vietnamese warfare.

In October 1967, Wergen, along with two of his brazen and most trusted Rats, finally achieved their well-deserved notoriety after they spearheaded the immense and critical tunnel-destruction operation near Saigon (now Ho Chi Minh City), dubbed, AKRON III, which would prove to severely impede the notorious North's Tet (lunar new year) Offensive of 1968, though they didn't know that then.

Staff Sgt. Thomas Wergen and Saigon's Marshall - 1968 (now Ho Chi Minh City)

In awe of their accomplishment, a U.S. Army artist drew up an insignia and had the emblem, along with their story, widely distributed — especially to some key places back home in the United States. The time had come to recognize these Rats for what they were — courageous, superior and uncommon warriors. It was soon after this event when Wergen's unit was to be officially designated "Tunnel Rats" and awarded the insignia by the battalion commander at a small ceremony in Di-An. (Only they proudly wore this small badge on the upper right sleeve of their fatigue jacket.)

From then on as the exploration and denial of enemy tunnels became a broadly significant and tactical defensive strategy for the U.S. effort, Wergen's Rats gradually became one of the most actively summoned units in Viet Nam by the American high command. Although most military divisions had men who would volunteer to work the tunnels when found, Wergen's unit was regarded as the best and most professionally equipped to deal with anything out of the ordinary "hole in the ground," with their keen exploration techniques, deadly demeanor and high-explosive demolition expertise.

Independent nomads, yet dutiful and dependable, the Rats would constantly travel to any given battle hotbed to carry out their missions whenever their priority had been attained—usually focusing on the most essential and dangerous of operations that engaged in direct confrontation with the enemy.

And while they were aptly named the "Tunnel Rats" for obvious reasons, they were also regularly found themselves embroiled within conventional warfare in major campaigns around South Vietnam such as *Operation Manhattan* at Long Nyugen, and fighting alongside the South Vietnamese at the Special Forces Camp at Loc Ninh when it was ferociously attacked by a battalion of the North Vietnamese Army (NVA).

Tunnel Rat Insignia patch

Yet still, tunnel denial was not all the direct combat they were involved in. The *Rats* were often plucked from their already death-defying duty for even more harrowing combat. This included finding themselves being chopper-ferried with the 5th Group 1st Special Forces "Hatchet Squads," or on a tedious traipse deep into enemy territory bent on a strategic, covert warring mission—dubbed "Sneaky Petes."

A few times they were sent to join the highly classified and lethal force called the Military Assistance Command Vietnam – Studies and Observation Group (MACV-SOG) for special projects across the border.

The mundane name of *Studies and Observation* was a mask for this fierce "commando" division of special fighters made up of the different armed services, who operated in deep secrecy all over Southeast Asia, most especially where they *'weren't,'* —according to

America's geographical political deployment policy, which was frequently declared and published by Washington. These *'weren't'* places included North Vietnam, Laos, Cambodia and even *China*.
(Note: The random China missions—which the *Rats* were *not* a part of—were carried out to sabotage munitions trains and obtain proof that Beijing was supplying war supplies to Hanoi. Unfortunately, most of these missions were fatally unsuccessful.)

MACV-SOG saga was declassified in 1984 and received the following Presidential citation for bravery in 2001:

"The *Military Assistance Command Vietnam - Studies and Observations Group* is cited for extraordinary heroism, great combat achievement, and unwavering fidelity while executing top secret missions deep behind enemy lines across Southeast Asia. Pursued by human trackers, and even bloodhounds, these small teams out-maneuvered, out-fought, and out-ran their numerically superior foe to uncover key enemy facilities; rescue downed pilots; plant wire taps, mines and electronic sensors; capture valuable enemy prisoners; ambush convoys; discover and assess targets for B-52 strikes; and inflict casualties all out of proportion to their own losses."

Sgt. Wergen comments: *"MACV-SOG Training was conducted in South Vietnam. Standard procedure was to have two weeks of intense physical and mental training followed by an actual mission behind the enemy lines. However, without being formal members and with little time and our services needed, we skipped the first two weeks and just went behind the lines the first time that we were called upon.*

When we were temporarily assigned to them we mainly intercepted enemy convoys and supplies, or provide information as to where and when they were coming. We spent weeks mapping and mining the Ho Chi Minh Trail and blowing up convoys and trying to just watch and figure out where all the supplies were coming from.

Our overall vision of this part of the war was kept very narrow because of its covert nature. We were assigned to a group, given a mission and told to follow until called to do our part. I'll never forget the first mission when an officer taught me how to walk silently through the jungle, and when this sergeant said 'don't speak until asked.' Hell, we didn't even breathe loud. We were simply told to follow orders, learn what you can as fast as you can, keep your eyes open your powder dry and perhaps you'll stay alive. It was a thrilling ride, but then, we made it back."

Wergen strongly suspected that many of the special force missions he was involved in were trickled downward through the command — *only* orally, non-traceable — from Commander, General William Westmoreland because of the heightened political sensitivity that existed in the United States. (He would find out — firsthand.)

Wergen and his Rats were continually amid the "thick of it" — literally, kill or be killed on almost a daily basis. Here one day and gone the next, Wergen's Rats became known as "the ghosts of Di-An," their home base (pronounced zee-on). They would be shuffled from one hostile hellhole to another — sometimes twice a day. And usually with no clear landing zones available, they would be chopper-rappelled through the dense jungle canopy and hauled back up when their perilous work was completed. With their assignment having been carried out, the *Rats* would usually arrive back to base camp more combat-hardened, silent and disheveled, resembling weary chimney sweeps, wearing filthy tatters that had once been a fresh uniform whenever they had left camp to begin their mission.

Wergen served in Southeast Asia from July 1967 to October 1968 when the fighting was at its heaviest. He is pleased of being awarded with the *Good Conduct Medal* for exemplary and efficient performance and more proud of being decorated with the *Bronze Star Medal* for meritorious and heroic achievement. Yet he feels most honored earning the *Combat Infantryman badge* (CIB) awarded for thirty days of sustained ground combat while serving with the Special Forces.

Also during that time, soldiers riding in combat aircraft earned *Air Medals*. Basically, one medal equaled twenty-five trips, or fifteen actual air assaults. The *Rats* spent a lot of time in combat airships and earned these medals—Wergen estimates about fourteen.

Wergen and his Rats also received a lot of unfavorable attention from the enemy during his Vietnam tour. While realizing the ravaging and specialized force of the Rats, the high powers of the North offered valuable rewards for their hides, especially Wergen's, because of his leadership and detonation skills. The bounty was without avail, as Wergen would survive his war tour—albeit wounded four times, including spending time in the Long Binh hospital after being blown-up while riding in an APC which hit a mine (he was the only survivor.)

Choppers arriving with Special Force Squad to pick up Wergen and his rats at Lai Khe for a covert mission across the border into Cambodia

So sit back and turn the lights up bright to ward off any dank darkness and follow Sgt. Wergen and his "Elite Tunnel Rats" as they trudge the steamy jungle trails, seek out the enemy and descend into the jungle abyss during one of the most treacherous and censored warfare periods in history.

Author's Comment: Although the basic facts, anecdotal action and places of Sgt. Wergen's account remain a matter of public record, the author has taken the liberty to dramatize to add cohesiveness and interest. Also, many names were changed for reasons of privacy protection; however, Staff Sergeant Thomas E. Wergen's was not. RS

Chapter One

Di-An Camp of the 1st Infantry Division — Bien Hoa

On a muggy, steel-gray dawn in early October 1967, Staff Sergeant Thomas E. Wergen gradually awoke with no particular agenda in mind — except to stay alive. Lying in his bunk sluggish, with a slight hangover, he wiped the beads of sweat from his forehead with a soggy towel hanging off his bunk frame. The first night back in his rack after days in the jungle battlefields was welcome but hadn't done him much good. Even after a long hot shower and a few beers the night before, he still felt exhausted and anxious. He couldn't remember when he'd last enjoyed a solid night's sleep, regardless of where he'd collapsed.

He stared up at the crude asbestos roof of his makeshift living hooch as his usual first-waking thoughts came to mind, *would he make it through another day in this miserable hellhole?* Would he survive the treacherous jungle elements…mortar fire…sniper bullets…land mines or any nearby road booby traps that might have been set overnight by the village Viet Cong? With a gloomy sigh, he wondered what lay in store for him today. Would he be in another APC that gets mined? And would he be as lucky this time — living through it. He thought about last month's spell in the Long Binh hospital; and how he was the only lucky one of the eleven soldiers.

Maybe duty today would be easy and he'd only hold some training briefings on demolition tactics, or tunnel denial to the new recruits who'd just arrived. Or if he was really lucky he'd manage to get the day off and only have to do minor stuff like schlep supplies or ammunition onto convoy trucks bound for some war site. Or maybe he'd only have to help tote foul body-bags to whatever transportation would be used to send yesterday's unfortunate casualties on their last journey home.

But then again, perhaps today his agenda would end up a little tougher, and he'd be picked up and carted off to Bien Hoa Air Base to join a 5th Special Forces Group to proceed on another crucial and highly covert "Hatchet Squad" mission *anywhere* in Southeast Asia to ambush and eliminate *enemy* convoys, or to provide information as to where and when the convoys were coming from. *Anywhere* on the Ho Chi Minh Trail might even be in Cambodia or Laos — where they *weren't* supposed to be.

Wergen cracked a thin smirk while thinking about the limited geographical war policy that Washington kept politically spinning to the American people back home; and how the Army spread lip service of "no troops in Cambodia" stuff for the official press; and that only warplanes were allowed across the Eastern borders of South Vietnam, or North of the demilitarized zone. If only the U.S. network news cameras could follow him around for a week or so…then the entire world would really know where they 'weren't.'

But he understood why the U.S. powers did the spin with half of the country now believing that the American involvement in Vietnam was a mistake; and 50,000 anti-war protesters marching on the Pentagon in Washington.

Wergen comments: Of course we soldiers knew about the growing protesting in the United States, but we couldn't worry about that. We could only do what we thought was right and what we were ordered on any given day. And we didn't have much choice anyway.

Or perhaps his day might be worse yet, and he'd find himself being air-ferried off to another jungle hotbed that hadn't yet been totally cleared by the allies, to be rappelled from an open hatch of a hovering chopper through the dense canopy of the 50-ft. trees, hoping and praying there wasn't any need to dart about to avoid enemy fire. But usually that was not expected as "Charlie" would then have *violated* one of Ho Chi Minh's ten rules of warfare to be the first to shoot — they were to be a listening post, not a shooter.

And perhaps much more terrifying this time, it would be his turn to be designated "first out," helplessly strapped in a harness when he was the first to reach the hidden jungle floor to find out if there *was* enemy lying in wait at a listening post: North Vietnamese troops lurking in the bowels of the jungle foliage as "lookouts," close to possible landing zones waiting for these awkward American missions to materialize. And if Wergen didn't give the coded line-tug or yell upward that things were clear, he might be left to fend for himself. The slick had no choice but to assume an evasive stance because the pilot commander would have to think of the others — perhaps leaving the unfortunate soldier to fight to the death, if he were still alive, that is. In this particular ruthless jungle warfare the survival code was simple: don't end up in enemy hands while still breathing.

Wergen and partner heading for 5th special Forces mission

Wergen had heard what the edgy NVA soldiers do to "first out" when they knew they were discovered — it wasn't a pretty sight. Charlie knew no one would follow and they wanted to ensure these men wouldn't be around to provide any more heroics. Worse, if given time, sometimes Charlie made sure the body was barely recognizable as the limp, but heavy harness was swinging upward while the chopper made its way clear to avoid any ground fire assault. Charlie knew they made their point well with this horrific action. Even the hardiest of U.S. forces who witnessed the harness-carnage would be quite reluctant to carry out this type of mission again — or at least be one of the first out.

Wergen's face stiffened as he gathered his energy and awkwardly swung his body to sit up on his bunk. Yet perhaps today he would face the most dreaded of all, surviving whatever terror, he might encounter in the next enemy war tunnel, or tunnel clusters he and his small group of brazen men would have to blindly explore and destroy — unfortunately, this was his main duty lately.

Although he realized he had volunteered for this, he knew it would be just something else anyway. And he did his duty well.

Yet, regardless of whatever he faced today, he knew it wouldn't be straightforward. His daily warfare was never easy, regardless of how he hoped it would be. The brass now routinely called on him, knowing he could be assigned to do anything. And there was always something distressing going on with the war escalating at a torrid pace. Being an intelligent and decisive man of few words, or outward complaints, Wergen only wanted to complete the duty his country asked of him and make it back home alive.

Wergen rubbed his stressed temples, contemplating the word *alive,* like never before in his life. That word now brought chills. *Weren't his odds of living out the day wearing thin?* he wondered, reaching for another towel sitting rumpled on his footlocker. He faced thoughts of death routinely now. Wasn't his turn near?

He wiped away more trickles of wet from his face as the sun began to fall behind the gathering rain clouds, transferring its relentless broil to a stifling humidity. He rolled the towel and put it behind his neck to soak up the wet. He squinted, regrouping his thought. *Weren't the grim statistics climbing? Why not him?* He'd heard that over 15,000 men had already lost their lives here; 9,000 this year alone. *So when it came to kill or be killed,* didn't the enemy have the same chance as him? They're human. They have weapons. They want to survive. *Would today be the day his turn came up to take the "final wrap"?*

He shook his head, ridding the chilling thought as he reached down along the side of his bunk and fumbled for the final cigarette sprouting from a wrinkled package lying on the rough cement floor where he'd left it last night. He lighted it, and again laid back, placing an empty beer can on his chest for the ashtray as his prepared to finish dealing with his usual life and death realism that always festered inside him to begin his day.

How his life had changed since he had shipped in from Ft. Benning, Georgia where he had been comfortably teaching demolition tactics to the Vietnam-bound troops. He thought he was safe from harm's way by being a professional chemist and needed for teaching, not combat. But then he got his new orders. Everything went to hell with his pat life. Even his long-time girlfriend, Cheryl, had virtually left him when he got the ship-out news. She couldn't stand waiting around for a "potential ghost," she had told him. But Wergen was expecting this as she was a San Diego State college activist, who rejected the whole Viet Nam thing. She felt the conflict was unjust, and thus she would regularly protest. Wergen could never convince her he was no conscientious objector; that just wasn't in his makeup.

An uneasy Wergen about to be rappelled into another "hellhole" for a special mission.

And even when Wergen received his Vietnam papers, he thought he would pretty much avoid the ground combat and perform his duty only in the heavily US fortified training bases. While hardly one to shirk his responsibilities, Wergen had still wanted to avoid finding himself in a kill-or-be-killed situation if possible—as most would. So be the hope—stay far enough away from the enemy-peppered jungle; far from the bloody hand-to-hand combat.

But it hadn't turned out that way. He glanced down at his calloused hands and grimaced with a churn in his stomach as he flexed the blistered forefingers that had already killed...with a rifle...pistol... and the blowing up of enemy convoys—indirect death, but still the same. Whether it had been dutifully right or wrong he still loathed the thought, like almost all the soldiers who were stuck in this confusing and vicious environment.

Closing his eyes, he recalled last month when he had found himself temporally attached to the Mike Force amid a major enemy offensive of "Junction City" in Loc Ninh. He had been called in to support a unit of the 5th Special Forces to prepare the camp with explosive defenses for an expected massive assault by Viet Cong and the NVA besides helping to train a battalion of South Vietnamese soldiers.

The resulting fierce battle at the base wasn't supposed to turn out the way it did, directly involving him. He had only been sent there to set up explosive traps and flares around the perimeter for defensive purposes, to train the South Vietnamese in demolition and then be air lifted out before any attack. But he just couldn't get out of there in time. And so again, it was either kill or be killed. Yet he wasn't planning to be pulling triggers with the rest of the soldiers. How every day and night for several days Viet Cong sappers and snipers made a major attempt to onrush and capture the camp, while the allied forces heartily defended in astonishment as the onrushing enemy were stopped dead, piling up like cord wood outside the base perimeter as though they were committing suicide.

****

Sgt. Wergen anxiously looked up from the various explosives and scanned the man-made barren track set about a hundred yards from the Loc Ninh base camp entrance. He sensed the surrounding jungle was beginning to "crawl" with more than the natural jungle vermin of poisonous snakes and spiders.

Wergen comments: I hadn't been in Vietnam long, but now more than ever I realized what I'd been told at briefings. Be cautious – always assume you're only a gunshot away from death. I really appreciated that warning at Lock Ninh on those days.

Even with the heavily armed 5th Special Force, and a battalion of South Vietnamese Regular Army guarding the perimeter and watching over him intently, Wergen worked nervously. He knew he had to prepare for the worst of attacks as he covertly fixed a small detonator cap (mouse trap devise) on the final U-picket fence post that supported the rolls of razor-sharp barbed wire.

Wergen comments: I knew this setup would do the job. If the Claymores and trip flares at the far edge didn't stop Charlie this would be a helluva final deterrent. The Special Forces really appreciated these mouse-trap devices. This was a nasty way to go. It's called "shooting the wire." If the masses of onrushing enemy rose to overwhelming, the traps were detonated by trip-wires inside the camp. The coiled razor-sharp wire barrier would spring to life and slice through the oncoming enemy like hot butter — shredding them. It was a final effort to stop a massive assault but it created a major mess of human carnage.

The only problem was that the setup wasn't that noticeable but there was a twenty-five percent rule in effect. In other words, one had to assume that twenty-five percent of the South were Northern sympathizers, so we had to keep this vicious snare quiet so the enemy wasn't tipped off. Actually you had to live by that rule concerning everything you did.

With dusk falling, a heavily guarded Sgt. Wergen took a final walk around the camp, double checking his explosive handiwork and reinforcing any wire traps around the perimeter where necessary.

With his job done, Wergen was going to leave the next morning but he didn't make it out of there in time before the fighting started. The NVA threw at least one battalion at the camp as the fighting was intense until the north ran out of soldiers. They didn't have to shoot the wire as Charlie was stopped at the first fence about 100 yards out.

Wergen hadn't been sent there as a shooter or a savior, but only to mine and booby trap the wire but he was caught up in the battle until things settled. Finally he was air lifted out and taken back to his home base: Di-An.

Chapter Two

DI-AN Camp of the 1st Infantry Division — the Big Red One

Sergeant Wergen rose from his bunk and shook his head realizing how lucky he had been at making it through the Lock Ninh battle when he had been so exposed while planting and detonating the barbed-wire traps at the base perimeter.

He turned and peered out through the slatted screen at all the buzzing and ongoing military activity realizing why he was always so busy. Di-An was a hectic place. Not only was it headquarters and base camp of the 1st Infantry Division (the Big Red 1), but also the home base of the 101st Korean Tiger Division, 168th Combat Engineers and the 27th Land Clearing Task Force — his main employer of tunnel denial lately.

Wergen comments: Di-An was in the hub of military activity of South Vietnam. The base was about a mile square and housed approximately 25,000 troops.

It was located just northeast of Saigon and between two rivers Song Saigon and the Song Dong Nai. Close by, slightly south and west was Bien Hoa a major air base — along with Tanh Sa Nuht in Saigon.

Bien Hoa was the headquarters of the 5th Special Forces, and many American fighter aircraft squadrons and the South Vietnamese air force training center.

Wergen looked down at the remaining few cans of beer bobbing in the large tub of tepid water that the night before had been teaming with ice and brew. He turned toward the roughshod bar and the small refrigerator he had managed to commandeer from supply. He was pleased that he and his rats were afforded a special hooch setup, but then, why not? He and his rats did special things.

Fully awake and feeling better, he smiled, wondering if their special hooch-girl, Hoa, would show up today to clean and visit with him. She was a pretty Vietnamese girl, barely seventeen, but over there they grew up quickly. She spoke good English and had grown into a special friendly relationship with Wergen and the Rats.

They all liked and respected her; especially when she offered fresh daily village "Charlie information" that aided in providing the Rats more safety — in particular when they were called on to sweep the nearby village roads for booby traps.

Wergen's Hooch—notice maps and other amenities

Wergen thought about his *Rat* team and looked over at, "Cowboy" Pvt. Robert Cornell lying in the adjacent bunk, still zonked out from all the beers he had shared with Wergen the night before. Wergen turned to the other corner, seeing that *Rat*, "Monkey Man" Sgt. Charles Dunning's bunk was empty. Probably find him on the way to mess, Wergen thought, as he bent down, reaching into his foot locker for a fresh set of fatigues.

After showering and lethargically dressing, Wergen slowly made his way out onto the bush-trail, cutting through the steamy vapor toward the chow hall. He looked up at the sky wondering about the rain. He was glad the rainy monsoon season was coming to an end, with some of the major mud holes drying up. Maybe he'd get some duty up in the central highlands where it was cooler, he hoped. But he realized now that it was drying up, he and his rats would probably be assigned more mapping duties of the Ho-Chi-Minh trail with the Special Forces into Cambodia.

Wergen comments: The Monsoon season in Viet Nam is from May to October, which made it extremely difficult for the enemy to move supplies and equipment down the Ho Chi Minh trail, mostly carried by humans through the mud and rain. But with things drying up they would begin to move more easily.

The trail began at Hanoi and went for 1,500 miles south through Laos and Cambodia. So it was now part of our job to find and map some of these routes (trails) close to the South. We'd then mine them and also

blow up any expected convoys as our air force couldn't really see the activity because of the heavy foliage and tree canopy. It seemed like a never ending job. Of course, it was.

I understand the first U.S. air strikes against the Ho Chi Minh trail had begun in late 1964 and the trail was continually bombed by American jets when they could see what was going on. But obviously bombarding it really didn't do much good in stopping the incredible flow of enemy soldiers and supplies from the North; after each attack, the damage along the trail would be quickly repaired, mainly by female "construction crews."

Hoa – Vietnamese House Girl

Wergen passed the small shack the rats had converted into a "trophy room" and wondered if he'd gather anything new for the wall today. Would he ever!

Entering the nearly empty mess hall, Wergen looked around for Dunning. Not seeing him, Wergen figured he was hiding somewhere wearing off his hangover. Grabbing coffee and a gob of scrambled eggs, Wergen found a seat at an empty table over in the corner and sat down.

****

Pushing his empty tin plate aside while absorbed in idle thought, Wergen finished his third cup of coffee. He suddenly looked up, noticing an excited soldier coming toward him while animatedly waving a piece of paper.

Wergen knew something important must be up, because anyone who approached him under usual circumstances—knowing his typical morning, no-nonsense mood and common brooding—did so cautiously, not abruptly.

While anxiously handing Wergen the scribbled note, the soldier blurted that an urgent message had just come in from the 1st Brigade Akron III commander. Wergen nodded as he looked up at him with quizzical eyes, accepting the paper.

While Wergen looked over the message, the courier filled in the blanks, promptly chattering that the radioman from the Engineer Brigade of the 9th Infantry Division, had just called with a frantic, "Found something really fucking big," message from a dense forest at Phouc Tuy Provence east of Saigon, where a critical U.S. search and destroy mission dubbed, "Operation AKRON III" was underway.

Wergen poses inside base camp "trophy room"

The radio dispatch explained that the brigade had earlier encountered numerous "Charlie" sniper attacks but had managed to adequately flush them out of hiding — easily eliminating them. And while doing so the troops had uncovered what they believed was an unusual cluster of tunnel entrances and the preliminary reconnaissance had suggested the underground find was immense.

The courier then said the radioman had excitedly reemphasized that something really fucking big had been discovered and the commander was sending word that they needed the professionals there — now! The courier finished telling Wergen the commander's slick will be waiting for him and his unit at 09:50 at the base landing pad

Wergen nodded and looked up from the message then at his watch as he quickly rose and left the chow hall knowing he had no time to waste. Not with a high-command directive of that nature on his tail.

Wergen comments: I had been in Viet Nam for a few months and was well into the Tunnel Rat business. In fact we had discovered and denied quite a

few lately. But I sensed from the message the commander sent me that something was really different about this tunnel find.

Entering his hooch, Wergen found his two best trained and trusted *Rats*. Cornell was sitting on the edge of his bunk coming out of last night's alcohol-induced stupor; and Dunning was by his bunk dressing after a shower, slightly more alert.

"C'mon Cowboy…Hey Dunning, let's go…C'mon get ready," Wergen uttered strongly, as he strapped on his .45 and bayonet. "We're going to Phouc Tuy Provence … Akron III."

"What? Aw bullshit," Cornell grumbled rhetorically, "we just got fuckin' back from a mission." He rubbed his aching head, but knew it was useless to argue.

Wergen chuckled over Cornell's usual morning complaining, then said, "Yep, but I understand the 9th found something big out at Akron III this morning…sounds really important. The commander wants us there. He's even sending his own slick to pick us up."

Wergen notes: We lived through continual tension day in and day out – and once our current mission was completed, we would frequently indulge in alcohol, from wherever we could get it – the only "stress reducers" we allowed ourselves. No drugs allowed – period! Waking up with hangovers was not unusual for us, and it was certainly no excuse for us to miss duty. In fact, sometimes it made us more "effectively ornery."

After we gained our notoriety and respect, we could have beer sent to us wherever we happened to be with only a simple request. However, with alcohol or not, we were never "out of sync" while on a mission, especially when denying a tunnel. We had to have our natural senses buzzing when we were doing a tunnel exploration; and we had to be especially alert when encountering the enemy, or setting the hair-trigger explosives during the tunnel destruction phase.

Carrying their sawed-off M2A1 Carbines and small back pack of supplies, the rejuvenated *Rats* left their hooch, heading for the landing pad and the revved up and waiting slick to whisk them off to the brigade site, AKRON III. Wergen and his elite team of Tunnel Rats were going to work—and they would find out, stunning work.

Chapter Three

Phouc Tuy Provence East of Saigon—Operation AKRON III

Sergeant Wergen and his rat team arrived at the AKRON III site and exited the chopper in wonder and filled with enthusiasm. They spotted the mighty bulldozer with an oversized blade (Rome plow) completing its relentless rumble through the dense jungle growth carving up and clearing away the last of the heavy foliage within the estimated boundaries of the vast tunnel area that had been discovered. The Rats were also overwhelmed by the sheer number of people milling about the area.

Wergen comments: The Akron tunnel cluster was incredible at first sight. I stood there next to Cornell and Dunning and we were all scanning the top layer of bared earth, which resembled a gigantic slab of Swiss cheese. There were all kinds of entrances. The radioman was sure right. This find was big.

The Rats had gained enough experience to immediately know this was no ordinary war tunnel and they had correctly sensed the magnitude of the discovery. Yet, they had no way of knowing at the time that they were standing over the largest tunnel complex constructed for enemy housing and storage of weapons ever discovered in the history of the Vietnam war.

The *Rats* officially took over command of the tunnel inspection and destruction mission after receiving a short briefing from a couple of brigade soldiers who had originally gone into the tunnels for initial reconnaissance. They had found some small weapons, multiple passageways and soon realized that the tunnel seemed to go on *forever,* and that this venture was far more than they could handle and had emerged.

After splitting up the *Rats* cautiously and randomly examined some of the entrances. Experiencing no sign of enemy activity, they came to believe the complex was virtually, if not completely deserted. The rats figured that either the NVA (North Vietnamese Army) had quickly abandoned the area upon the arrival of the

AKRON III troops, or the enormous underground compound had been constructed to serve only as an enemy staging point for future planned attacks, or as a refuge for quick retreats.

Wergen notes: At this point we were months before the TET offensive and had no idea that this was probably why the tunnel complex had been constructed. Of course, we would know then that this discovery was a stroke of luck as it would have made a real difference to the North, perhaps even the difference to them winning Saigon, instead of losing.

Rat, Pvt. Robert Cornell's favorite position outside of a tunnel

The *Rats* were eager and ready to find out what lay beneath them. Each with a weapon drawn and a makeshift mine probe, (An aluminum rod attached to a wooden handle that the Rats would use to cautiously poke around for buried "things" that could kill them — as a blind man with a cane.) Wergen, Cornell, and Dunning slowly proceeded down the first entrance and into the unknown to begin their preliminary but cautious exploration.

Wergen comments: We gave up on small silenced weapons because the bad guys didn't know they were being shot at. We carried .45's and sawed off M2A1 carbines and cowboy carried a colt .38 revolver. Sometimes we had earplugs, but your ears still hurt when you fired. But the results were usually the same: you only needed one shot most of the time to clear the tunnel because Charlie thought you had a howitzer in there.

Carefully making their way down the tunnel passageway while cautiously maneuvering their probes, they came upon a trap door in the flooring. As Cornell readied his carbine, keeping a standing, outward watch, Wergen and Dunning kneeled down to concentrate on every inch of the door, quietly discussing the possibilities of what type of booby or human trap might await them as they painstakingly worked open the wooden hatch. Leaning back on their calves, they looked at each other in surprise as they came to realize it was an entry to a lower level of the tunnel — now a tunnel known to be at least two levels deep.

With their adrenaline and curiosity raising to fever pitch the *Rats* wanted to go down and explore this level, but they were professionals and closed the hatch. They knew their most essential task at this stage was to estimate and map the global perimeter of the tunnel complex to determine the boundaries in order to quickly set up enough ground-level security to enclose the tunnel outskirts. Everyone already realized this would be no one-day job. And most important, they couldn't chance *only believing* that the tunnel was clear of enemy and then that night have Charlie slip into the tunnel from an unguarded far-side entrance and be lying in wait for the *Rats* on their next search.

Wergen comments: At this point we had to reasonably trust that the only way to enter the tunnel system was from the surface entrances. But of course, until we reached the bottom level we really had no choice but to assume that premise.

Continuing to gradually move stealthily along the wide passageway, the *Rats* stopped when noticing areas where the packed earth in the tunnel walls sported different shades of color. Probing further into the bamboo roots and soil, they discovered that the NVA had built side compartments the size of standard rooms — clever construction, albeit sloppy craftsmanship.

One of the first compartments contained hundreds of weapons including SKS sniper rifles and numerous 9mm sub machine pistols. Although their adrenaline flow was now mounting from their exciting discoveries, they were growing concerned with the overall complexity of what they were facing. They weren't quite sure what to expect next. After a hurried whispered conference, it was decided they needed backup troops to come down and follow up behind their advance, because these side compartments could be harboring enemy troops who could possibly trap them.

Wergen comments: Usually when we were inspecting tunnels we didn't want any "outsiders" to interrupt our methods, but in this case it was different. We wanted someone to watch our backs so we could really concentrate on what we were finding. Yet support for tunnel searches was always volunteered, as this type of perilous duty was never ordered.

A gigantic D-9 Bulldozer sporting a jagged Rome-Plow-Blade, being unloaded for jungle "clearing work" (below).

They swiftly doubled back and made the request for volunteers. Because Wergen's *Rats* were leading the way, acquiring that backup support proved easier than anticipated when a few anxious soldiers nervously volunteered to enter the tunnel. Inside, some remained stationery near the entrance, while some followed slowly behind the *Rats*.

The *Rats* had also recognized the great distance they had advanced when they were inside the tunnel and hence requested the brigade commanders to significantly expand the security perimeter above ground. This scurrying around to secure the tunnel—above as well as below ground—was now the sole activity in the area for *miles around.*

****

Finishing their first day of initial exploration, the Rats emerged from the tunnel feeling somewhat more comfortable. After a daylong search the Rats were now reasonably confident of their first impression that the tunnel levels were unoccupied, or at least they felt their chances were good enough that they should concentrate only on non-human perils and would holster their weapons—only one would wield a carbine. However, as always during the first stages of a tunnel discovery, the Rats had no way of knowing what to fully expect until they actually descended into the bowels of the tunnel for a thorough search. And again, with this tunnel, they knew there was at least one more level below the one they were on.

Wergen comments: This was the most dangerous element of tunnel rat duty – keep taking things one chance-step further, or deeper, based on gut instinct and utter courage, I guess.

Enemy food supplies found in Akron tunnel "Kitchen." (Notice from where the Rice had originated.)

One issue was becoming clearer to the *Rats*: they would need more supplies and definitely more support troops than first anticipated to surround and firmly secure the area before they could safely finish the work on this enormous underground complex.

After discussions with the brigade commander and requesting the additional troops, they decided to wait until the fresh light of dawn to continue their search, rather than get caught "down there" after nightfall – they would already be facing enough uncertainty without the added cloak of surface darkness.

That evening, while the *Rats* were gathered with a fresh infantry lieutenant inside a makeshift campsite close to the tunnel, a bullet suddenly pierced the relative calm, scattering sparks from the camp fire.

"Goddammit," the startled lieutenant cried, as they all dived for cover. "I thought this fuckin' place was secured."

He wanted to quickly send out a patrol to flush out the sniper(s), but Wergen and the rats had experienced this activity before when coming up on a valuable enemy find. And they convinced him that the sniper was either "a really bad shot" or just, messing with their minds and they best just stay out of his range and be left alone, because the incident could easily prove a deadly trap for the searchers. They quickly squelched the fire and separated to slip into the darkness for a place to try to catch some fitful sleep.

****

The next morning a call for reinforcements triggered a frenzied "gold rush" effect as the stunning tunnel area became known. The perimeter was soon overwhelmed with non-brigade and a throng of visitors consisting of military writers, photographers and artists, to generals and other heavy brass from all around the South. Yet Sgt. Wergen's *Rats* remained unobstructed and were fully in charge of the tunnel and extremely enthusiastic to begin laying major damage to the enemy's war effectiveness, by swiftly implementing the immense AKRON III tunnel search-and-destroy strategy. The initial plans were put into place and there was no more time or effort to squander.

With adequate troops and armored vehicles now on site, the brigade force was able to create a heavily armored 1000-yard perimeter to keep anyone from entering or leaving the area—friendly, or otherwise.

Meanwhile the *Rats* began their second cautious and methodical descent deep into the earthly abyss to commence exploring the vast and remarkable layers of networked underground passageways while the engineers and troop backups followed behind them to start hauling out the war booty.

With the tunnel orientation becoming more straightforward and more secure as they further prowled the passageways, the *Rats* now carried bright floodlights finding more side rooms and nooks and crannies used for various living purposes. This was only the beginning of the amazing results they were about to turn up as they began to more accurately assess the magnitude of their underground find.

For days, Sgt. Wergen, "Cowboy" Cornell and "Monkey Man" Dunning completed the front work, clearing the way of booby traps and discovering yet more levels and more side compartments. With the *Rats* safely taking the lead, the troop apprehension had been replaced by excitement and amazement. The armed volunteers willingly followed behind, emptying out the tunnel as they advanced. Now most everyone wanted to experience being in the tunnel—even a couple of Generals.

A general being helped out of tunnel

With little sleep, no bathing, their blood-soaked fatigues in tatters from the grinding scuff of the stony earth, the *Rats* spent eight grueling days and nights of intense effort to search and lead the clearing of the entire tunnel; only the adrenaline rushes that kicked in when they found more concealed compartments and encouraging cries from above ground would keep them going. Adding to their frustration, they had to bypass some of the entrances into the small cubicles that were considered too dangerous to tamper with because of suspected sophisticated booby and punji man traps. Even the *Rats* didn't want to meddle with them—unfortunately leaving their contents sealed and forever unknown.

Finally, with all the patience and perseverance they could muster, the *Rats* began to make their way to the last unexplored section at the very bottom of the tunnel complex. They were so deep into the earth that even their radios ceased to function, rendering them helpless if they found trouble and needed assistance from the "outside" world. Regardless, they continued their descent until suddenly a stench of death began leading their way.

Reaching the bottom, the *Rats* were astounded as they peered past their powerful light beams that illuminated the colossal man-made void. They had uncovered a ceremonial burial chamber— piled high with the skeletal remains of North Vietnamese soldiers, hundreds of them. This incredible find proved to be a fitting end to the "search phase" of their mission, as they turned and began their journey back.

****

After an exhausting search with a charting phase that exceeded a full week, the Rats rested in the warm afternoon sunshine, still overwhelmed as they assessed the extent of the Akron discovery. As they had first estimated, the overall tunnel system proved massive.

The incredible passageway system exceeded *three miles* from the first entrance to the far end of the tunnel. The cavern depth measured *eight* levels in some areas. Various levels were spacious enough to literally drive jeeps and trucks through. They estimated the all-inclusive underground structure had been designed and constructed to accommodate approximately 5,000 enemy troops; including a rudimentary but complete dental office, hospital equipped with an operating room, eating area with a kitchen and sleeping quarters.

Among the startling cache of captured and removed arsenal were two 75mm French Howitzers, hundreds of 9mm sub machine pistols, U.S .50 caliber machine guns, SKS sniper rifles, mortars, and the list continued — numbering over 2,500 weapons. On the third level, where the heavy artillery was stored — howitzers, mortars and anti-aircraft guns — had passageways so wide that when two men stood with arms stretched outward they still couldn't reach the walls. The ceiling was over six feet high, as most of the men would not have to stoop while traipsing through. The third level contained the kitchen area and main living quarters. The level below housed the hospital and the dentist office.

Wergen comments: This dentist space was cleverly designed so that the dentist sat on a small side seat next to a makeshift dental chair and pedaled the drill unit, which was attached to some slapdash contraption consisting mainly of bicycle pedals and a chain and sprocket.

Every alternating level had a huge, manually-operated fan to move air into the lower reaches and the North had shrewdly used rabbits and squirrels to dig "natural" air vent outlets by binding a topless cage against the roof. The frustrated animal would then burrow an almost undetectable opening to the surface. One of the strange things about the tunnel was the lack of lighting. Only a small number of oil lamps and candles were found, mainly in the hospital and dentist area, with a few stored in the main living quarters. The tunnel occupants must have moved around mainly in the dark.

At the end of inspecting the tunnel, Sgt. Wergen was sure they had missed as much as they had uncovered, but this was wartime, and the Army was operating on a tight schedule. They had to end the tunnel inspection and move on with its destruction.

Some enemy weapons captured in Akron Tunnel

Due to the sheer vastness of the tunnel, they now faced the enormous logistical "headache" of the destruction phase. It was easily recognized that the usual undertaking of destroying the tunnel complex by planting and detonating tons of explosives under the earth was simply too much effort in itself for this situation, and the demolition could prove ineffective. Therefore, Wergen and the Rats along with the brigade commanders swiftly devised an ingenious plan of employing tear gas powder wrapped in detonation cord, along with high explosives, and finally flooding the caverns.

More captured Akron tunnel enemy weapons

When the tactics of the plan were detailed, they calculated that the assault was so massive there weren't enough high explosives in the country to meet the obliteration, requiring them to promptly fly in additional supplies from Korea.

Finally the strategy, supplies and manpower were in place for the tunnel annihilation phase to be carried out. For two full days close to a hundred men carried and strategically placed various explosives along with 10-pound bags of CS tear gas powder wrapped in primacord into the tunnel according to plan.

Wergen comments: Explosives and flooding are good for denial, but the real stopper hear is the tear gas. When the ignited cord disperses the CS tear agent throughout the tunnel – into the walls – the toxin remains potent for decades. No one can get near them.

Meanwhile, the brigade had brought in numerous gigantic water pumps housing oversized flexible fire hoses, and stationed them at the river, close to the tunnel entrances. When the pumps began chugging the water, the hoses were slowly "wormed" into the tunnel entrances reaching to the base of the tunnel. It's estimated that it required over two million gallons of water to flood the bottom levels, while the middle levels were charged with the tear gas powder, and the top three levels were packed with heavy explosives placed every ten- to twenty-feet.

Wergen comments: Having the river close by was no stroke of luck. AKRON, like most all of the larger tunnels, was strategically constructed close to water to provide a place to rid the excess dirt. In this case tons. Most all of the soil that was unearthed would be discarded into the river so as not to leave any traces of tunnel activity to be discovered.

When the explosives and CS tear gas bags were detonated, the top levels of the tunnel caved inward, converting the once titanic living complex into a gigantic mass of gas-infested sludge. The destruction and final denial of the largest enemy tunnel ever discovered in Viet Nam was now successfully accomplished.

For tactical insurance, the brigade set up a large guard around the area. But of course, no NVA troops or Viet Cong militia would ever arrive. They had obviously observed the colossal search and final destruction through the jungle canopy as it was being carried out.

****

The American high command, along with Washington, felt quite fortunate that the tunnel had been discovered and destroyed; especially *after* the *Tet Offensive of 1968 began,* when the tunnel complex could have been manned to support the Northern forces that were to attack Saigon and neighboring provinces. Based on the flag that was found, the tunnel had most likely been built and operated by a NVA supply battalion with the offensive in mind. (Their red flag can be found in one of the photos with the weapons.)

Intelligence later informed Sgt. Wergen that the North Vietnam government was outwardly furious over losing such a critical stronghold. And that they had learned who had masterminded the destruction of the tunnel, most likely a result of the dreaded 25% traitor rule being carried out by Southern sympathizers. Further, the North swiftly put out the word: bring in the *Rat's* hides to gain high-command favoritism and if Sgt. Wergen's head was delivered, there was a reward of 100,000 piaster for the lucky eliminator. (This was about $10,000 USD, a fortune at that time for a Vietnamese soldier.) *Wergen comments: I suppose if this were accurate the main thing I find disturbing about the bounty was that they specifically named me...probably because I was the designated Rat leader with the high-explosive demolition expertise. It was disturbing because it was easy to find out where my base was – although I was rarely there.*

****

After the destruction phase, the exhausted and grimy-looking *Rats* rested while somewhat irked because it wasn't long before almost all of the big brass from the area arrived to have their photos snapped as though they had something to do with the tunnel denial accomplishment. To further aggravate the *Rat's* ire, some would even hold up a captured weapon as though they had crawled their way into the God-forsaken abyss and had hand-plucked it from the enemy themselves.

Yet, in actuality, Sgt. Wergen and his trusted *Rats,* Cornell and Dunning were the first three to clear the tunnel so the troops could safely enter and haul out the bounty while bragging to the press. As usual, the *Rats* were deep underground and mostly unseen with little glory while struggling with stressful darkness and booby-traps while dodging fire ants, spiders, scorpions, snakes and poisonous centipedes.

Wergen and his *Rats* would gradually end up chuckling over all the hoopla. Their humor and a few congratulatory beers would help them adjust to their annoyance. Besides, the *rats* really had no time to reflect because soon after some limited sleep, a jungle-shower (the pouring of only two, rationed helmets-full of clean water over their bodies) and some borrowed fatigues, the *Rats* quickly found themselves being shuffled onto a well-armed chopper for a flight to another hotbed area dubbed "Catcher's Mitt" — a vicious no-man's land with known concentrated pockets of enemy located South of IV corps, Northeast of Bien Hoa on the Song Bo River.

Every day the allied forces would face constant spurts of sniper fire originating from the numerous tunnels, which were heavily camouflaged and extremely difficult to locate, much more to attack and destroy. Therefore, the US cavalry unit was increasingly frustrated during combat while attempting to hold onto the area. So the commanders decided that the tunnels had to be effectively eliminated, and sent word to the Akron site that they needed the professionals there — now!

The Rats had only begun, but they had already gained their fame. This immediate demand for Wergen and his *Rats* would go on non-stop, throughout Wergen's tour in Viet Nam. After "Catcher's Mitt" the Rats would be ferried to the "Iron Triangle" above Xuan Loc (pronounced swan lock) north of Saigon, which was heavily occupied by the American 11th Armored Cavalry Regiment after a major Spring, 1967 military offense had been conducted by the United States and South Vietnamese forces to clear the area of North and Viet Cong divisions. That operation had been dubbed *Operation Junction City*.

Wergen comments: We felt like migrant workers going from field to wherever the brass would send us. But the time sure went by fast.

****

As the military chopper raced atop the jungle canopy heading for the "Catcher's Mitt" war zone, a weary Sgt. Wergen closed his eyes and leaned his head back against the cabin partition as he began to wonder why he *had* volunteered for all of this while still in college. What had he been thinking that glorious, sunny spring day in San Diego in 1966 when he had enlisted? What…what…

Chapter Four
May 1967 — US Army Infantry School, Fort Benning, Georgia

Chemical Staff Specialist E-4, Thomas Wergen sat stunned as he again looked over his orders that had just arrived — Viet Nam bound! He was puzzled? Wasn't he considered valuable property here at Ft. Benning after just being sent here from Ft. McCllelan, Alabama where he had graduated eighth in his class from the army school for advanced training as a chemical staff specialist? Hadn't the long diligent hours he spent successfully learning chemistry, biology and nuclear physics as well as demolitions training that led up to him being the student company commander — as well as an instructor at this U.S. Army infantry school — provided him solid and safe state-side duty.

Still perplexed, he looked up for thought, wondering further, wasn't he valuable here helping to train and graduate infantry bound officer candidates (2nd Lieutenants)? How about the ones slated for artillery duty, and those for the chemical corps? Weren't they depending on his main area of expertise and coaching before deploying to Viet Nam?

Yet Wergen had no idea at this point that one of the demolition specialties he was teaching at Ft. Benning involving the tactics of tear gas CS powder and primacord detonation would make him one of the most recognized "war-active" Vietnam tunnel rats within a year.

Wergen comments: The maneuver dubbed "Tunnel Rats" had first come to being in January, 1967 during the major Cedar Falls battle in Viet Nam's Iron Triangle. That's where they discovered the vast enemy underground networks, and basically that's when America began to make tunnel denial a regular defensive warfare operation. So we were gradually making tunnel demolition and CS tear gas tactics part of our teaching agenda at fort Benning. Of course I had no idea then that I would soon become one myself.

Wergen sighed and slid the order papers back into the manila envelope, deciding that regardless of where or what he was doing now, the war was raging in Southeast Asia. Of course he would go without objection. Just the same as the men he was teaching.

After all, he had realized on that serene and sunny March day in 1966 when he enlisted at nineteen this perilous Viet Nam duty would probably come — and why not him? He was courageous with high intelligence and a youthful strong physique. Moreover, he was now a specialist teaching demolition tactics to Army recruits and future tunnel rats alike, so Wergen had all the attributes that the army needed. Why not put him to actual war use?

Rising, he stashed the envelope in his office drawer and decided he would put in for a month's leave before shipping out in July. He wanted to go home to Rosemead, CA and see all of his family just in case it might be his final chance; although he certainly wouldn't tell them *that*.

As he began jotting down his travel thoughts, he wondered if instead of enlisting maybe he should have remained at San Diego State and graduating as his long-time girlfriend, Cheryl, had pleaded with him to do. He was sure now she would go her own way. She wouldn't be able to withstand the worry if he'd ever return home — so many were ending up missing and dying over there. Hating the war, and distrustful of the politician's spin on what the fighting stood for, she was a consistent anti-war activist in San Diego. Wergen was sure his being called to Viet Nam would only solidify her negative stance.

Yet Wergen couldn't and *wouldn't* worry about that — it wasn't in his makeup, and he was in no position to settle down anyway. There were too many unknowns in his life right now. More important, he had no time to dither. His country was at war, and whether it was right or wrong it was his duty to serve. Subliminally, he kind of welcomed the chance he was now getting. And surely over there he would be kept sheltered on a well-protected base because of his unusual MOS (military occupational specialty) and training skills. He probably wouldn't even experience any actual combat, he thought, as he rose from his chair, suddenly growing excited. Yet still, this warfare experience would certainly help him grow and mature.

Yet Wergen had no awareness of how *soon* he would mature when the bullets were flying about and he would be in the middle of it all. He had no idea that soon after he arrived in Vietnam his MOS would change to *Combat Engineer*. And that he would be directly involved in the bloodiest, fiercest and heaviest fighting that would take place in South Viet Nam, North Vietnam and Cambodia during the entire war. He had no idea he would be sporadically assigned to the mighty 5th Group, 1st Special Forces during some extraordinary fighting, and would experience stealthy military undertakings that weren't especially publicized back home — undertakings in areas where US troops weren't supposed to be — according to the Washington administration spin.

And Wergen had no idea that soon after he arrived and was assigned to the recon division of the 168th that he would be riding with troops in an explosive-chocked APC that hit a mine. Not only would he be blown up, but he would witness ghastly carnage and death close-up, before ending up in the hospital (the only one who would survive out of twelve soldiers.)

No, Wergen had no clue that he was about to "mature" from being an army stateside-instructor into a hardened active combatant earning war medals and ribbons — jaded to a point of either kill or be killed on a daily basis shortly after waking. He had no inkling of what his sudden maturity process would soon entail — no idea whatsoever.

Yet before, he *would* be granted his leave from Ft. Benning and subsequently made his travel arrangements to allow him to visit all his friends and family in California, before going off to war with having no real indication at all on what hellhole madness he was about to face, and have to battle through, so to speak.

****

Specialist Thomas Wergen harbored no expectations that July day in 1967 as he nervously looked out the porthole window of the military chartered 707 airliner abruptly lurching upward into the muggy, jungle skyline. He was experiencing his first taste of hostile reality as their original destination of a repo depot (replacement camp) in Bien Hoa was being suddenly switched to Ton San Nhut (Saigon) when the plane had come under a heavy onslaught of enemy mortar and rocket fire.

At finally landing in Saigon, an uneasy Wergen and the rest of the new arrivals were loaded onto deuce-and-a-half troop transport trucks and taken to the repo depot at Long Binh post where he would be assigned to a specified unit somewhere in South Viet Nam. (Long Binh had the distinction of being the largest military base in the world at that time.)

Tired and anxious, Wergen lined up with the other arrivals (newbies) while the unruffled dispatch clerks perused each of their records to further assign them to their next in-country assignment—war bound. Wergen's turn came and he was temporarily assigned to a combat engineer force stationed there at Long Binh Post. The "maturing" game had begun and the first inning was over.

Wergen comments: I noticed that most of the dispatch clerks had no unit patch on their right shoulder which usually means they had no combat experience; and they were just assigning us to wherever they thought would be a good fit, after only a couple of minutes. That concerned me a little, and I got my first taste of Army personalization – not!

****

As the days passed into weeks Wergen was randomly and temporarily attached to a unit in charge of the Vietnamese laborers in the camp, while he hoped for more defined placement orders. Each day Wergen's crew would send out trucks and buses to the nearby villages to pick up and deliver the locals to work on the base—hundreds of them. And sometimes Wergen would drive into Saigon to pick up replacement troops for some of the armed groups. And sometimes he would just spend the day driving around sightseeing. Wergen was bored and discontented. Army life at Long Binh was ringing hollow and dull.

He also didn't relish living and sleeping so close to the largest ammunition dump in the world, which was getting targeted night after night by enemy mortar and rocket attack. Wergen began wondering about a better way to pass his days—but not necessarily safer.

One afternoon while sitting in the EM (enlisted men's) club, Wergen suddenly found his *better way*, and it would eventually pave his prominence throughout his tour. Someone at the bar told him about an opening for some tunnel rats in the *168th Engineer Battalion, Combat* based in Di-An, home base of the *Big Red One*.

Wergen's eyes lit up and his adrenaline rose. After giving a few minutes to "careful thought" he smiled and left the club, making his way to *Long Binh* headquarters administration to find out where and how to apply.

Wergen has it easy at first – Sightseeing in Saigon

Wergen comments: It may not have been one of my wisest decisions to date, but again, with my background, I thought I'd only be an active trainer for the Rats…I thought, anyway.

****

Specialist Thomas Wergen had the physical characteristics and the educational qualities they needed and he was promptly accepted, immediately welcomed and processed into service by the 168th Combat Engineers when he arrived at Di-An.

Wergen's tunnel-rat life at Di-An began slowly, although the duty quickly grew more motivating than his last assignment at Long Binh. At first he carried on reconnaissance work for the engineers, inspecting roads and bridges, helping them plan on how much gravel they would need to fill pot holes, or to determine if a certain road or bridge was adequately constructed to support a convoy, or a heavy troop movement.

Yet more dangerous, at times he'd be assigned actual convoy duty and be used to sweep the village roads for mines and booby traps while keeping a vigilant eye out for Charlie before the critical supply trucks could proceed onward after he rendered the way safe.

On one occasion Wergen realized mines were being repeatedly buried on a road close to the house of a suspected VC sympathizer. Wergen studied the pattern and became convinced the house owner must be allowing the VC to bury the mines, by looking the "other way." Finally fed up with the activity, one day Wergen noticed the house was empty. He set a block of C-4 explosives between the planted mines and the house and blew it all. The house was obliterated—coup de main. No mines were ever planted in that vicinity again. Without guilt, Wergen was maturing!

Wergen stands next to a house he obliterated because of a Viet Cong mine-planter living there.

He also occasionally worked with the *27th Land Clearing Task Force*, a hearty group of soldiers—seemingly impatient and fearless. They drove the monstrous D-9 dozers with the giant Rome-plow-blades, relentlessly clearing the jungle and rubber plantations of foliage and anything else that might get in their way while they thundered onward to uncover tunnels and any other hazardous elements. Sometimes as they worked, they inevitably flushed the enemy out of their hidden burrows.

Wergen recalls on one of his first missions with the 27th, they were unearthing a lot of spider (sniper) holes, and evidently one of the VC snipers became so upset over his concealed mound being run over by one of the 25-ton dozers, he jumped up behind the roaring beast and started awkwardly shooting at it with his SKS weapon. The operator ducked down at hearing the shots pinging off his machine and calmly reached for his Thompson sub-machine gun, turned half way in his seat and quickly deposed the crazed sniper into a bloody heap. The operator then turned back and continued on with his plowing, as though this were a common occurrence, which it was—another foreshadowing chapter of Wergen's new role in Viet Nam.

A U.S. War photo of an M113 Armored Personnel Carrier (APC), dubbed the "Green Dragon"

Wergen would also help deny the tunnels that were found by the 27th and he was becoming more enthused about this endeavor; as he had found more of the action. He felt now he was beginning to earn his increased army pay— albeit a meager reward for such a perilous hazard on his life. But he had to remember...he had asked for this.

Unfortunately, one day Wergen found more action than he had wanted. On a multiple-tunnel destruction mission in late August 1967, he and eleven other soldiers were confidently riding atop of an M113 Armored Personnel Carrier (APC), dubbed the *Green Dragon*. This heavily assault-laden vehicle was loaded with 800 pounds of C-4 explosives when it suddenly rolled over a Russian anti-tank mine that ignited right under the engine. The ACAV was demolished.

The actual demolished M113 APC Wergen was riding on after it hit a land mine.

Wergen, who was resting just behind the driver was blown well above the jungle canopy and landed about 100 yards down range.

He remembers the sensation went from wretchedly hot and noisy to feeling a cool breeze on his face as he crashed through the tree branches and landed on a huge pile of plowed brush, writhing in painful agony.

At hearing the explosion, soldiers from the 27th working on a clearing-rise, above the tree line had seen him hurdling through the air and immediately rushed to find him before the enemy might — especially if he were still alive.

Although still in one piece, Wergen was disoriented, badly bruised and for a couple of days he remained in great pain and deaf before being air evacuated out to a hospital in Long Binh where he recovered his health and his hearing over the next few weeks.

As Wergen lay in the hospital being the only survivor he could only think of the other soldiers on the APC who hadn't lived. How lucky he had been. And he had now matured further to a chilling rationale: For the rest of his tour he would definitely have to kill or be killed — period. He would need no further maturing.

Wergen comments: This was a real wake-up call for me. It was no more "cowboys and Indians" game. I don't believe I ever relaxed again while in Viet Nam, unless I had a bunch of beers in me.

After Wergen recovered at Long Binh he swiftly returned to Di-An and the intensifying war where he learned the commander of the 168th battalion was set on developing a name for himself. He had increased the visibility of his recon unit by making them *more tunnel rats* then reconnaissance specialists. Wergen also learned that during wartime, personnel positions open up quickly. Having enough time with his current ranking, and with his proficient abilities using explosives and CS tear gas powder to deny tunnels, Wergen strongly stood out. Therefore, the commander gave him a Sergeant rating as a Recon/Tunnel Rat leader and changed his MOS (military occupational specialty) from Chemical Staff Specialist to Combat Engineer. Wergen was now officially in charge of the tunnel Rats. His pay was again raised and his real war had officially begun.

Chapter Five
September 1967—Di-An Base—Tunnel Rat Development

Sergeant Thomas Wergen was readily but unceremoniously accepted as the leader of a current tunnel rat squad that appeared disjointed, loosely organized and undisciplined. They had a reputation of going out on missions now and then, seemingly only when they felt "up to it." Wergen realized that although these rats were limited on experience and passion they weren't short on guts and gall. And when they did go on assignment, they performed their duty without much thought for the consequences of a mistake—doing the best job with the techniques they knew.

Yet their nonchalant attitude over such an important enemy deterrent as tunnel denial bothered Wergen; and while he studied the men and their haphazard routines, he decided things had to change—now! He decided they needed to become committed, confident, dependable and methodical—now!

Wergen comments: I dunno...I suppose I felt that if we were going to risk our lives for each other we should shape up. Or maybe I had watched too many war movies. Whatever...I knew things had to change. And it was now my responsibility to change them.

His group came with a grizzled Private, "Cowboy," Robert Cornell, who Wergen quickly realized was the most experienced Rat of the bunch. (He was dubbed "Cowboy" because he loved riding in jeeps behind an oscillating M-60 machine gun like a cowboy on a horse shooting Indians.) Cornell was a hard-bitten case and had been in the country a long time, already earning six or seven campaign ribbons. Wergen liked Cornell and decided he would strongly rely on him. And it would turn out to be a wise choice.

Another less-experienced one in the group who Wergen immediately also favored was "Monkey Man" Jim Dunning (dubbed because of his agile ability to scamper in and around tunnels like a monkey). A no-nonsense type who Wergen decided would also be one to rely on—again a wise choice. Wergen, Cornell and Dunning would make up the crux of Wergen's team throughout his Viet Nam tour as a tunnel rat leader.

There were a couple of part-time sergeants in the group: one a prudish type of guy who doubled as a driver for the base brass and another man much too big to be an effective *Rat* for Wergen's style. They both spun out quickly as the organization began to purge and jell. Sergeant Wergen had taken Charge.

Wergen teaching new tunnel Rates demolition at Di-An

Wergen comments: I soon learned there were two types of personnel, "Mr. neat-and-clean" who hated getting dirty, and then the old vets like Dunning and Cornell who liked the action and didn't play well with others. I wanted more men like them — guys who didn't mind getting "dirty." The others quickly rotated out.

During their beginning period they began inspecting the local tunnels and honed their techniques of searching and destruction with the leadership of Cornell's past experience and Wergen's demolition skills. The *Rats* developed keen methods with only hand tools, courageous instincts, determination and small weaponry to rid any enemy that might be unfortunate enough to be in the their way — man or ground creature. The Rats were always watching each other's backs — as this was their most critical mandate.

They employed no sophisticated technology or tools like today's unmanned reconnaissance aircraft with its high-accuracy radar, or thermal-guided cameras designed to detect and photograph underground hot spots — ala enemy sitting around a camp fire while holed up in a large tunnel. No, these *Rats* only had simple weapons and their wits.

When entering and while inside the tunnels they basically relied on all their senses while searching for the enemy or booby traps of all types and descriptions — moving, or not. They were constantly handicapped while meandering and stealing about in the dank darkness, almost always having to depend on touch, feel and lots of warfare intuition.

Most always on discovering a new tunnel, no flashlights could be used during the initial inspection because that only made the *Rats* more of a target than they already *were*. For their beginning search, they had only their natural night-vision to quickly develop once they were "inside the hole."

The *Rats* would tote various weapons during their search-and-destroy operations. They first carried a .22 automatic pistol, which was equipped with a silencer to reduce the risk of damaging their eardrums while engaged in a shootout inside the tunnel. But they soon learned that the enemy was usually wielding heavier-duty weapons and the *Rats* were returning ineffective "pea-shooter" fire. As a result, the 22's were quickly scrapped in favor of sawed off .30 caliber M-2 Carbines. On especially dangerous occasions they toted silenced .45 caliber "grease guns," which were the most effective. Yet many times these vaporizers proved too large and bulky to be lugging while crawling around in the tunnels under typical conditions.

Wergen comments: The decision on what weapons to carry varied on the circumstance. But, of course, the more lethal the weapon, the more effective we were. I'm confident that many times Charlie quickly left when they saw us coming, and what we were packing.

Some tunnels were easy to locate, some were not. Rarely was there any surface indication of the tunnel's underground architecture. But the majority of the tunnels were the wriggly and crawly type, 10- to 20-feet long and 2- to 4-feet in diameter—man-sized burrows to conceal snipers and their paltry living supplies and weapons. These tunnels were mostly dug by the North using a basket in one hand, and a short-handled hoe to sort of rake the soil into the basket. They would then hand the basket back from person to person to dispose of the soil at the end. On small jobs during the rainy season Charlie could just spread the dirt onto the earth and within two weeks the small mound would turn a natural green and meld in as part of the landscape.

Yet some tunnels were complex and incredibly designed — typically with multiple entrances that were well camouflaged to thwart U.S. military invasion. They were large enough to adequately accommodate large throngs of Viet Cong troops for prolonged and fierce warfare aggression. "Air ducts" in the bigger tunnels were usually small and usually undetectable at ground level. The *Rats* learned from the AKRON III mission that these ducts were cleverly developed because they were naturally burrowed through the earth by animals.

Wergen comments: One has to remember, the Vietnamese people were at war since the 40's beginning with the Japanese. In 1967 we may have been at our infancy of tunnel denial, but they certainly weren't so at their tunnel development. They were seasoned masters.

The type of tunnel soil used was laterite, rich in red iron and aluminum and when exposed to the air would turn as hard as concrete (laterite was also used for road surfacing). Because of this soil strength the only place the Rats ever found timber or wood in a tunnel was around the entrance or down below in trap doors.

Wergen comments: In over 900 tunnels we never found any type of shoring necessary to support the innards, even in the Akron tunnel which was eight stories deep.

The tunnels were discovered in many ways; sometimes by allied troops accidentally stumbling across them; or sometimes when the masking foliage was unexpectedly removed during construction of a military base camp or a temporary airfield. Yet most of the enemy's significant tunnels were "sniffed out" through the proficient efforts of the highly trained section of Army engineers called the 27th LCT (land clearing task force), which Wergen was assigned to.

To clearly uncover the tunnel surface area, the LCT operated huge 25-ton caterpillar dozers equipped with an oversized, trademarked, 2.5 ton cutting blade called a *Rome plow* that replaced the standard flat blade. Specifically built, the blades were quite sharp and beveled along the bottom edge. It took little time to lay the jungle bear with unrelenting swipes from this monstrous machine—clearly exposing the tunnel entrances.

Once the tunnel entrances were uncovered, the answer was *not* "whiz bang" with a few lively grenades or any other explosive pitched swiftly down the hole and "presto," that was it—over and done with. Unfortunately, ridding the tunnels was hardly a straightforward coup de main venture. The North was much too shrewd and heinously creative to render tunnel denial that simple. To make things more complicated, the South and the *Rats* were facing two war enemy factions.

Rome Plow at work near Saigon

The North Vietnamese Army (NVA) was a conventional force, much like the U.S. Army. They were the *obvious* adversary, well-equipped, uniformed, and moved about in standard formations, traveling in standard war vehicles.

Rome Plow aftermath – no mercy

Yet perhaps the more feared faction, were the Viet Cong who were like the civilian resistance fighters of World War II countries. They were inhabitants of South Viet Nam but covert supporters of the North and were largely indistinguishable from peaceful villagers.

Wergen comments: We weren't facing conventional warfare with meagerly-armed, rice-paddy farmers here, even though travelogue photos had that scenario appear as such. The Viet Cong were guerilla-cunning and well equipped martially by the North. And worse, we were intruding within their backyard, which they knew and understood well. They were damn good at their job — and could also dig damn good war tunnels.

Some Viet Cong factions interwove and at times fought with the NVA but—dressed like civilians—they mostly sabotaged American advancement, killing as snipers, carrying and harboring enemy supplies, growing and supplying food and other things that could be done stealthy to support the North even while under the watchful eye of the Americans and South Vietnamese army. Being at war continually since 1939, they were quite experienced.

Wergen's Rats as a team had learned tunnel-deception tactics early on. Some tunnels were set up only as dummies—shallow, and stuffed with hair-trigger explosives like short-fused hand grenades and anti-personnel mines. Consequently, if any tunnel deniers were explosive-careless while dealing with any of those tunnels, the aggressive maneuver would backfire, to put it mildly. (The rats called this the kfb scenario—or *ka fucking boom!*) More than once the kfb blunder *was* executed by a hasty and inexperienced tunnel rat chucking grenades into a newly discovered, yet uninspected tunnel, proving grim results.

Wergen comments: One unit working the Iron Triangle wanted us to train their own rat team. We spent three days in an intensive training class of do's and don'ts—especially not to throw a grenade down the hole before you enter and inspect it; especially smoke grenades which will eat up all the oxygen. And more important, you never know what explosives might be in the hole. So rule one, never just heave a frag into a tunnel.

The next week a few of them went out to search a tunnel and one of them who obviously missed the lesson tossed a grenade into the first hole they found. They happened to be standing over Viet Cong land mine storage. KFB! They were all instantly killed. After that, we swore off training.

The Rats also knew that any given tunnel might contain a tethered American POW, which of course, always dictated extreme caution while proceeding with any inspection and destroy phase. And there was always a possibility that the tunnel contained vital enemy supplies, or some type of key intelligence—including a potential North prisoner who was much more valuable alive rather than a heap of bloody shreds.

So consequently, the *Rats* virtually never knew what actually lurked down *there* besides the distinct probability of booby traps, punji man traps and poisonous vermin.

Wergen recalls on returning to Di-An from a tunnel mission where days before he had been bitten by a huge green spider about the size of a teacup saucer. The bite area was quickly developing a festering infection that appeared potentially gangrenous. Wergen immediately made his way to find the base doctor who was from Boston, and was bitter and angry because he had been drafted and had no patriotic desire to be there.

When Wergen approached him with his arm out at the medical building, the doctor was standing in the doorway flipping a scalpel in the air sporting his usual surly attitude. Saying nothing, he looked at Wergen's arm and immediately motioned for a medic to swab the area with alcohol before the doctor quickly made a cross incision. He then swabbed the wound out with a wooden Q-tip before peppering the cut with pungent sulfa powder and stitching it up. He did all this while administrating no anesthesia and while Wergen was still standing outside the doorway refusing to flinch.

Although Wergen was satisfied with the brusque treatment he was upset over the doctor's manner and his overall attitude, along with everyone else on the base. As Wergen left he told the doctor that if he ever saw him on any U.S. street he would run him down. The doctor knew Wergen meant it.

Wergen comments: Soon after, a few of us forced the doctor to go into the village orphanage to treat the kids because of their sores and other assorted maladies...no one was happy to be fighting over here, but you couldn't treat your war buddies like crap. Most of us felt we were all in this together. He sort of shaped up afterward.

So regardless of the horrific elements that may lurk down there such as the enemy, booby traps, poisonous vermin, any tunnel—particularly ones with passageways—had to be thoroughly examined before denial could be carried out. Thus formed the chief standard of the *Rats*—first cautiously investigate, and then react accordingly and decisively.

Chapter Six
Fall 1967 – Di-An Base – Into the Tunnels

Sergeant Thomas Wergen and his rats had jelled as a team and were working coherently in the fall of 1967. Tunnel denial was evolving as their main duty. They trusted each other and had developed solid and methodical tunnel strategy.

Sergeant Thomas Wergen entering Iron Triangle tunnel as "first in"
(U S War Photo)

The *Rats* usually employed at least three-man teams during their initial search. They all had their specified tasks, but again, their fundamental priority was to constantly keep an eye on each other's backs during this gut-wrenching phase. It was top priority. They *had* to depend on each other. For this reason, no new candidate could join their squad unless all agreed. In this work, they had to know that they would still be around at end, because of trusting someone behind them.

Wergen comments: When you first discover an unexplored tunnel you get that adrenaline rush that so many people thrive on. And then when you drop into the hole you are totally scared – virtually breathless for a moment. But then you realize you've made it this far and the adrenaline hits again while you gather your wits and proceed with your job.

Of course tunnel inspection is frightening, yet believe it or not, I was a hell of a lot more scared when we were bivouacked out in triple-canopy jungle with the special forces; many nights it was so dark you couldn't see your hand if you put it two inches from your face. At least in the tunnel you had this kind of cocoon that you could mentally pull around yourself for protection, but not out in the jungle with all the creatures and the enemy lurking around. It was darkness you can't even imagine. Goddamm scary dark!

The most delicate and anxious of tasks was being the *first in* to a newly discovered tunnel. They would take turns on handling this perilous duty. Not only was he responsible for *seeing* what was up ahead, but he also had to carefully scan and probe for explosive tripwires at the entrances before he led the rest of the rats into the tunnel. There was no time limit put on this part. The first-in also concentrated on finding other devious traps such as unusual deep-angled niches in the sidewall where a deadly King Cobra might be waiting; his tail secured with a tie and stake. Coming face-to-fangs with this ornery creature while unprepared could obviously lead to a ghastly fate—or at least one that would slow you down and wreak havoc on your routine, actually for all of them.

The second Rat followed behind, checking the sides for hollow spots or loosely covered accesses leading to other tunnels, while the third man had the responsibility of staying a bit further back, checking the top and bottom bases, searching mainly for false openings. The Viet Cong would sometimes install trap doors in the flooring, triggered to spring open directly behind the unsuspecting invader who had just crept past. When sprung upward, some doors were cleverly designed to remain steadfast to entrap the invader, rendering them helpless. Cramped and unable to turn around, it was only a matter of time before their life-sustaining air would run out, along with their sanity. Other trap doors were designed to suddenly swing open, allowing the enemy to pop up behind the intruder like a "jack in the box" brandishing a deadly ambush—which was usually a bayonet or a bullet.

Regardless of what traps or deceptions the Rats might encounter in the tunnels, they could never let their guard down. They realized there would always be something new and terror-filled for them to confront—compliments of the north.

Perhaps the most anxious times the *Rats* experienced during a search were when they'd enter a larger tunnel and find forks in the passageways. The team would sometimes *have* to separate and follow each route while adjusting their eyes to the darkness, and their ears to the stillness, desperately attempting to detect any sights or sounds of danger. (Again, rarely could flashlights be used here, because the beams made them ideal targets.)

If the tunnel system happened to be circular, the *Rats* knew they would eventually meet up with each other. Yet when they began, they had no idea if the tunnel network was designed as a circle, or who they might be approaching—and when. It may or may not be the enemy. It may be one of the Rats. Regardless, there would only be a split second for them to decide their choice of action, and that the decision had better be the correct one. Fortunately, these types of tunnels were few.

After the tunnels had been thoroughly inspected and whatever chores serving the U.S. interests had been completed, the *Rats* would move swiftly to obliterate the tunnels, usually with high explosives. But if none were available or the tunnel too large, they would set ten-pound bags of tear gas powder, looped with primacord (detonating cord) every twenty or thirty feet along the tunnel passageways. When the detonating cord was set off the powerful force would disburse and solidly embed the powder into the tunnel walls where the noxious effects would remain for approximately twenty years.

Yet whatever method was employed for destruction, it was ensured that human use of the tunnel was virtually denied forever—this time compliments of Sergeant Thomas Wergen and the rest of his "Tunnel Rats."

****

Wergen's *Rats* gradually gained notoriety from their war-tunnel effectiveness and began getting "order-calls" to go all over the country to clear and deny tunnels—so many calls that they needed more rats.

They recruited by word and radio to other units for volunteers who wanted to be part of this elite team; volunteers who would be regarded as growing in stature as tunnel rats who would command respect. Surprisingly, they ended up with a lot of candidates to choose from—but few made it.

Wergen comments: One man we recruited was Wally "Weasel" Cartner from the Midwest. He was so skinny and limber he could almost walk through concertina wire without ever getting a scratch. We sure liked having him with us.

During one routine tunnel mission near Cu Chi, the *Rats* had "Weasel" with them, and they found a tunnel with a small entrance that descended on a steep angle and a long way down. He was the only rat thin enough to fit. So they tied a rope to Weasel's ankles with the other end tied to the jeep bumper and down he went.

With Weasel on lead Convoy duty. Note white sheet so U.S. Air power could spot them. (Also sometimes was an unwanted target for Charlie.)

With Wergen and Cornell staying above ground, they suddenly heard the muffled crack of gunfire amid the cries of Weasel to get him out! We started the jeep and quickly pulled ahead. Weasel came out of the ground fast, scraped and cut, but otherwise intact. He explained he had slid down and ended up right over where a group of Viet Cong were eating. He only had a .45 automatic with seven rounds and was desperately out gunned, hence the hasty exit. Before the rats left, with carbines in tow, they searched for the main entrance and couldn't find it so they simply blew the tunnel and continued onward.

Wergen comments: That was a strange one. I remember Weasel saying he got two of em, but we didn't hang around to really investigate. Once we knew Charlie was basically living in that tunnel, we just decided to blow it up with a few grenades down the skinny hole. I'm sure if nothing else it interrupted their chow time.

Wergen recruited and found John "Balls" Whitler, who was a

combat photographer. He was invaluable in many ways. Being a professional civilian photographer he knew the power of the camera and saved the rats probable demise on numerous occasions by being the "pied piper of Di-An."

Being attached to the *168th Engineers* out of Di-An, the Rats would sometimes find themselves entering extremely hostile territory for recon assistance operations or leading convoys up "thunder road" (highway 13) to Phuoch Vinh and Lai Khe to bring needed supplies. Whitler would come along to document and snap photos of the physical condition of the intended route to aid the engineers in making determinations of later travel or repairs.

Whitler had a Polaroid attachment to the large format-camera he carried and he would tote about twenty boxes of film. Most of the reconnaissance shots were taken of the areas which brought out lots of civilians—mostly children. Whitler would hand out some quick Polaroid shots to the kids so they could excitedly show their parents.

Innocent Civilians or Bomb planting American killers along Highway 13 (Thunder Road)

This ploy accomplished two things. First, the *Rats* would always find themselves surrounded by hundreds of kids, making them less of an enemy target, and second, this allowed them to move about the village in a seemingly random and incoherent manner.

Whitler and the Rats usually always achieved the valuable snapshots they were sent to capture, and would leave a lot of smiling faces on the little ones and perhaps angry frustration on the elders that might have wanted to eradicate Wergen and his men.

In fact, Whitler was so effective with his camera, the brass allowed him to build an air conditioned dark room where he could do all of his own photo development.

Wergen comments: I think Whitler's dark room was the only air conditioned non-com building on the base. So it also provided a great place for us to hide out with a few beers when we needed to "chill," so to speak.

Wergen in air-conditioned darkroom

So now Wergen's Rats were not only becoming masters of the tunnelways, but they were now adequately proficient with explosives in warfare so they would be tasked with de-mining the highway and leading convoys safely between base camps.

Yet de-mining had been another skill they had had to learn. None of the *Rats* were professionally trained in *explosive ordnance disposal*, or *mine operations*. (The closest to actual training was what Wergen had at chemical school.) But disarming explosive weapons involved many of the same types of fuses and detonator method, only used in slightly different ways. So Wergen became the EOD team leader and would eventually disarm over 200 mines and booby-traps. The disarmed devices then would be sent to the states to be used as training aids at the engineer school in Ft. Belvoir, VA.

Wergen's Hooch Number—steals movie Line ¶

In all, Sergeant Wergen ended up with a diversified bunch they dubbed the "dirty dozen," ala movie fame at the time. His group included all types such as a farmer, a welder, a combat photographer. And like the movie, their missions became increasingly publicized while they gained more of a reputation for being not only loners, but effective fighters as well.

They were housed at the Battalion Headquarters Company at Di-An, but Wergen's hooch was set away from others on the perimeter as they were considered a bad influence on the regular troops because they were allowed special treatment.

No one wanted to cross them, and the brass loved them.
****

Nearing the end of 1967, the reputation of Sgt. Wergen and his tunnel rats had grown to being one of the most effective group of units in the military, which would lead to triggering unusual calls from different Special Forces groups. One of the groups they occasionally participated with on covert missions was the MACV-SOG. At first, Wergen's Rats knew nothing about this special group or how you became attached — other than it was made up of professional and quite competent fearless fighters, usually operating on orders coming from General Westmorland.

Over time Wergen learned of the grueling training camp of the MACV-SOG and how many Rangers and other special force type soldiers had failed to make the cut in the three-week school.

Wergen comments: I probably would have also failed to make the cut under normal circumstances. But at that time and place our "training" consisted of only one day — meet the team you were joining and head out on a mission. Keep quiet and stay alive in real warfare — that was our real training agenda. I'm glad there weren't a lot of those missions...they were damn brutal.

The *Rats* were surviving and were now earning their standing for being combat soldiers as well as tunnel rats — in spades. This was also the beginning period of their diverse covert operations which led to further enhancement of their status.

In addition to their missions with the MACV-SOG, Wergen's Rats would be assigned to the Army's *5th Group 1st Special Forces* — specifically supporting the *MIKE Force*. They also found themselves on special missions with the *11th Armored Cavalry Regiment*.

Thus Sergeant Wergen and his *tunnel rats* were becoming the Jack-of-all "war trades." With their bravery, expertise and dedication they were now priming and preparing to perform their remarkable and horrific missions deep into the jungle abyss during the bloodiest and heaviest fighting stage of the entire Viet Nam conflict — 1968.

Wergen and his Rats were now deeply immersed in their new-found war—or perhaps *the war* had found *them*.

Chapter Seven

Catcher's Mitt — Northeast of Bien Hoa, River Song Dong Nai

Sergeant Wergen slowly opened his eyes as he felt the abrupt landing at his new place of deadly employ. The area was dubbed Catcher's Mitt because the shape of the river that runs along the southern and eastern perimeters of the zone shapes it to appear as a mitt. The region was known by the U.S. forces as a major concentrating area for the NVA units and formations that had moved down the numerous parallel infiltration trails and paths known collectively as the Ho Chi Minh Trail.

Wergen comments: The region was dubbed catcher's mitt for the area of location but those of us unlucky to be sent there for duty it was also dubbed catcher's mitt because every night the zone caught constant hostile rocket and mortar fire.

Weary and muddled, he lifted his head from the cabin wall and quickly dismissed his counterproductive thoughts about that sunny San Diegan day when he had enlisted. It was done... he was here. Now as yesterday, the day before and tomorrow, he only needed to concentrate on staying alive.

Battling the slamming heat and dusty odor through the open hatch, Wergen and his rats warily exited the chopper that had brought them straight from the Akron tunnel destruction site after only a few hours of sleep and cold-rationed food.

Trudging their way toward the makeshift cluster — that made up the 11th Cavalry headquarters — for their briefing, Wergen and the rats looked around at the parked jeeps and scurrying well-armed soldiers cautiously guarding the zone that the rats had been sent to support. The *Rats* had heard and now realized by seeing the tense activity that this was probably a strategic staging locale for the enemy and an ongoing gut-wrenching experience for The 11th Cavalry who were tasked with clearing them out.

Wergen would learn just how stressed the situation was from the welcome greeting he was about to receive. Approaching a soldier to ask for the base commanding officer (CO), Wergen was unceremoniously pointed toward a command track—an all-purpose carrier (APC) with an elevated top so the occupants could stand and move around freely. The tracks were also air conditioned to service the radio equipment and to provide comfort for the top brass who would set up control inside.

Surrounding the tracks were a few scattered tents and deep trenches. The area was bone dry and the U.S. soldiers had to basically live and sleep in underground bunkers for protection from the onslaught of enemy shelling—the rats would prove no exception.

Arriving at Catcher's Mitt, near Bien Hoa

Wergen walked over and curiously stuck his head into the lead APC hatch, while his two trusted rats stood behind.

The ranking Colonel looked up at him, barking, "Who the fuck are you guys"?

Wergen answered, "We're the tunnel rats sent here from Akron."

"You look like shit, what good are you?"

Wergen slowly explained they had just spent eight grueling days in the Akron tunnel and hadn't had a chance to get back to home base in Di-An for any type of recuperation.

"I see," the CO said, adding coolly, "I heard about that damn tunnel."

Wergen comments: It was not a comfortable greeting, but it was an effective way to make us really understand what a helluva situation they were going through here day after day. This guy reeked of stress.

Wergen stood silent as the CO promptly summoned the executive officer and told him to take a chopper to Saigon to get

Wergen and his rats outfitted with all new fatigues, weapons and whatever else they required for their upcoming tunnel work. He then told the rats to go and find a "big hole" to rest in until he called for them. The rats gladly complied as they quickly proceeded to walk around until finding a large suitable bunker before crawling in to snatch some much-needed sleep.

****

Somewhat rested and re-supplied—compliments of Saigon—Wergen and his rats learned at the CO's briefing that their initial understanding about the area was correct; the "Catcher's Mitt" region had been, and was now keenly strategic for the enemy. They were told the northern sector was farming country where the local village Viet Cong of Chanh Long, Hoa Loi and Chanh Luu would covertly supply food to the NVA and the Dong Kai VC regiment. And that the southern sector was dense jungle where the NVA could skulk defiantly, well hidden from U.S. aerial surveillance while they launched constant rocket attacks into the Bien Hoa air base.

Wergen comments: We didn't know it at the time, but the southern part of the area would be used as a main approach by the NVA and VC to get to Bien Hoa and Lon Binh during the 1968 TET offensive. Thousands were believed to have gone through this area to beef up their attacks.

The rats were further briefed on the mass production of enemy tunnels believed to have been quickly dug within the immediate area and had yet to be cleared—suggesting the tunnels were probably "easy pickings" for the rats to find and destroy them. Although Wergen wryly suggested that perhaps the "easy pickings" were the bad guys in the tunnels finding *them*.

****

For the next ten to fourteen days the *Rats* went to work. Unfortunately, there were no Rome plows with oversized blades to assist them as none of the *27th LCT* was available to be there at that time. And worse, the APC transport carriers the rats would consistently use to travel on were not able to penetrate the dense jungle.

They were occasionally aided by a couple of "big boy" M60 tanks fitted with dozer blades that would do a decent job of clearing away the bush to uncover the obvious tunnels found at the onset. But the *Rats* were mainly limited to being "on the outside looking in" before they would venture onward while depending on minimal aerial observations and available fire support from the gunships. This air protection, along with some small armed squads, probably was obviously the reason Charlie was kept at bay.

Although their tunnel denial work was mainly uneventful, every day still proved challenging for them. And as always, the days were especially unnerving as the *Rats* virtually ran themselves ragged inspecting tunnels to collect intelligence material, disarming booby traps and mines and then either having the tanks crush the tunnel, or they would blow them up if the tunnel had been effectively and tortuously burrowed. If the tunnel had multiple entrances the rats would apply the CS tear gas treatment, ensuring neither entrance was ever again useful.

Wergen comments: At night we would just lay in the enemy's back yard, hunkering down in some deep-hole bunker while experiencing major "shelling hell" from the NVA; and we had no major artillery or effective method to counter with…only patience.

Finally one day they were afforded time off for a bit of quiet time and rest. Ornery, tired and tested the *Rats* milled around the command track until the occupants broke for lunch. Wergen darted inside and radioed a buddy-connection in Di-An requesting their mail be sent along with some beer, if available. A few hours later a chopper arrived for the *Rats* bringing three mail-bags containing their mail, two 50-pound ice blocks and a couple cases of beer.

At first the CO became enraged at the rat's audacity, but soon cooled off and joined them drinking a beer, realizing the rats hadn't been back to their home base in weeks, and felt they were well worth the exceptional treatment anyway.

Wergen and his rats were pretty much left alone after that incident to finish their work. They ended up clearing and destroying sixty to seventy tunnels before they got word they were needed in another hot-bed area, *The Iron Triangle* — now!

****

Wergen sat reticent leaning against the track waiting for the chopper to pick him and his rats up to take them north for their next assignment. Of course they were glad to be leaving this area, yet they knew they were just being whisked off to another hell hole.

Cracking a thin smile, Wergen thought about how back in California he would occasionally see motor vans of migrant workers on the freeway being hauled to another farm to work. He felt he and his rats were beginning to symbolize those *braceros* being carted to wherever they were needed on short notice; only *not* to pick fruit on a friendly California farmland, but to jeopardize their total being at every turn and every yard of menacing earth they would face, or turn up.

But that ultimate danger was beginning to matter little right now. After only four months of tour Wergen felt he was already becoming shop-worn and definitely jaded. And why not? In this steamy enemy-infested jungle those feelings didn't take long to fester. He was neither excited nor distraught.

He didn't feel thrilled about being respected and praised for his unusual and harrowing heroic work of tunnel denial. He felt that *anyone* who stepped in front of bullets was a hero — above ground or below. And now thousands were in this jungle along with him, and they were stepping out and dying. He felt his warfare work of detonating talents and sheer bravery wasn't really any more important than theirs, but only different, that's all.

And he wasn't distraught about picking this unusual and different duty, literally on the go every day to ultimately seek out his possible demise — often times tantamount to suicide. Regardless, he steadfastly decided he would handle the pressure for another eight months, along with those other thousands of soldiers sharing and braving this Asian firestorm. And then, if he were lucky and still in one piece, he could go home. *He could do it…he was jaded*, he believed, squinting his eyes as he heard the loud chugging of the incoming chopper blades — onward!

Yet Wergen was wrong. He would find out ahead how jaded he had *not yet* become. He would find out he had *not yet* faced the worse of existing warfare which was about to engulf the heaviest and bloodiest fighting in the next year — 1968. He would find out how secretive and treacherous the duty he would be asked to do would become; facing complicated combat warfare results that would remain with him for the rest of his life.

Not yet twenty-one, combat veteran Sergeant Thomas Wergen was about to face a major transition in life he had no idea of, a transition he couldn't have fathomed even existed — onward!

Chapter Eight

Late Fall, 1967 — Binh Duong North of Saigon (Iron Triangle)

The Iron Triangle was a persistent stronghold of the Northern forces beginning when they were at war with the French in the 50's. And it was no different in their war with the Americans in the 60's. The area mirrored a massive beehive, encompassing approximately 115 square miles of sprawling enemy nests.

In January 1967, *Operation Cedar Falls* was launched in the Iron Triangle. It was a major offensive that included over 30,000 American and South Vietnamese soldiers to purge the NVA and Viet Cong from the area. The enemy realized their overpowered match and mainly slipped away into the jungle. This is when the pursuing Americans uncovered an extensive network of tunnels and basically recognized, and began the "Tunnel Rat" program of search and destroy (deny).

Then from late February through April 1967, a second major allied military attack in the Iron Triangle, dubbed *Operation Junction City*, was conducted by the United States and the strengthening South Vietnamese forces with the same purpose, of course, to clear the area of North Vietnamese Regular army and Viet Cong.

And as before, the main intent was to eradicate the concealed enemy pressure on Saigon and Tay Ninh province — heavily populated civilian areas. The chief tactic of *Junction City* was to drive the enemy forces into the open for easy kill-pickings by the superior American weapons from the air as well as in the jungle.

This three-month battle was one of the fiercest U.S. offensive campaigns of the entire eight-year war, which included the employment of massive American airborne operations. Within the first few days in February hundreds of U.S. aircraft sorties struck the enemy and over 230 troop transport helicopters landed to pepper the area with allied soldiers. Twenty-six battalions (25,000 men) of South Vietnamese and American troops comprised the overall assault wreaking havoc among the scurrying enemy, verifying the assault to be making a difference — at least, the U.S. powers believed as much.

As the intensity of *Junction City* gradually subsided, major elements of the U.S. infantry divisions, the 11th Armored Cavalry Regiment, and the strengthening forces of the South Vietnamese army gradually swung back toward Saigon to conduct another key clearing operation, dubbed *Manhattan*, now taking place in the Long Nguyen base area. This offset of supremacy left a basic but hefty skeleton of allied troops in the Iron Triangle to mop up and to strive to maintain a military superiority of the area.

11th Armored Cavalry insignia

Although the NVA and the Viet Cong were severely thinned as a result of the *Junction City* onslaught, the Iron Triangle remained a mass of enemy activity surviving mainly within the cloak of thick jungle foliage and deeply submerged in the miles of tunnels that had survived the attack. This is when and where Sgt. Wergen and his tunnel rats came in, immediately after their effort in the *Catcher's Mitt*.

Wergen comments: Although this was our first rats-call to the Iron Triangle, we would find ourselves here on numerous occasions throughout 1968, especially after the TET offensive.

This area was constantly a center of hostile activity, continually fueling the need for us to destroy tunnels and seek out the enemy to eliminate them. We did that in bunches, but the need just wouldn't ever go away – Charlie was relentless.

****

Wergen exited the chopper and began to think about Thanksgiving Day as he broke from the group and slowly wandered around the immediate bomb-pocked area to gather his "war wits." He had never been separated from family and friends during the holidays. *Wergen comments: Vietnam was a helluva place to be for my first time away on the holidays. But I wasn't alone. There were thousands of us there.*

Wergen stopped and raised his head scanning the far perimeter of the clearing. He had only been briefly informed on the expectations of him and his rats, but he quickly sensed why this area would be a critical stop on his tour especially since it was quite close to enemy infiltration from Laos and Cambodia.

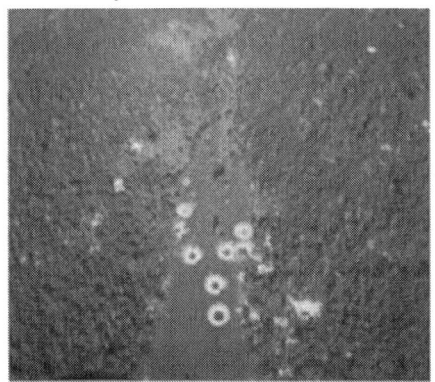

Rats Arriving at bomb-pocked *Iron Triangle* for work in late 1967

He was again in the thick of the action—perhaps never more so—permitting only a slim chance for any relaxation or recreation during the upcoming holidays. There simply would be no letup, day or night during this duty. Putting it into simple perspective, Wergen felt that wherever and whenever he caught some rest it was as though he lay in a projected path of a hurricane or a tornado wondering if he would be swept away while asleep. And when he was awake it was as though he was continuously dodging cars on a busy street *against* the light—only these drivers were out to kill him.

Wergen comments: It was nerve-wracking at best. And I knew it wouldn't get any easier. A battle with my nerves would have to keep me going. I knew I had to win.

Wergen sat on a tree stump to rest with no idea that he and his rats would discover tunnels that were even more astounding and even more precarious than ones he had already experienced denying over the past months. He had no warning that he would again shake hands with death in another explosion. And he had no cautioning that he would discover on one his later duty-calls to the triangle that not only was Charlie trying to kill them, but from what he knew if he were not thorough in his defensive tactics, weak and corrupt links within the U.S. ranks might end up assisting in that danger.

As dusk began creeping in Wergen rose from the stump thinking he had seen it all and tomorrow would just be another day in this miserable abyss, and he'd get through it as before. That's what he had to believe. He allowed himself no other choice. And he hadn't even seriously considered the menace of any local venomous nemesis, although he soon would.

****

Feeling restless after only a few hours of fitful sleep in another damp underground bunker, Wergen and his rats trudged through the early morning sunshine-slivered canopy just inside the jungle perimeter, swiftly finding their first tunnel entrance.

Cautiously readying his .45 in an arms-up position, it was Wergen's turn as "first in." He could see the tunnel entrance was constructed on a basic slope measuring approximately thirty degrees. It had rained a few days before and the laterite clay was hard and still slippery.

Wergen attempted to be careful with his footing, while keeping a keen eye out for any dire movement below and most important, any signs or markings of a booby trap. His stepping caution to no avail, his second step sent him onto his butt and into a tail-spin slide at a pretty good pace. Releasing his weapon, he knew he was defenseless but he had to put his hands against the side walls to try to break his fall as he had no idea what lie ahead — perhaps a punji death trap (in this case, needle-sharp bamboo shoots).

When he hit bottom Wergen was instantly relieved he wasn't facing any enemy perils but he shuddered at feeling a slither in his right hand. A snake! A giant centipede! Sitting frozen, he realized he had to hold tight to whatever was wriggling. He called up his initial safety relief to the rats, told them to stay put and decided to turn on his flashlight. To his horror he was gripping a huge black scorpion that was so long it couldn't sting his hand, as hard as the wriggling vermin was trying. Thinking quickly, Wergen put the light in his mouth, unsheathed his kbar (combat knife) and cut off the stinger and then the head before foisting the remains toward the dark corner of the tunnel.

Still shaking and flush with nervous anxiety, Wergen grew angry and frustrated from his fall. He found his .45 rose and only searched about 10- 15-meters inward before stopping. With not seeing or hearing anything or anyone, he just wanted to get out of there fast. He certainly didn't want to get into difficulty down there with perhaps only that one upward, slippery exit as his escape.

He hurried back to the entrance and yelled up to the rats to throw down a rope so he could be hoisted out. With Wergen safely at top, they all tossed a gas grenade in the tunnel and looked for any signs of other openings within close proximity. Seeing no one or anything worthwhile to further investigate, they blew the tunnel with more explosives and moved on.

****

The days passed without major incident, which simply meant none of the rats or any close associate was maimed or killed during their tunnel denying tactics. They were just too cautious to make mistakes—so far, anyway. They had to be. They ran into the enemy on a couple of occasions lurking in or near a tunnel and the guarding Cavalry soldiers or the rats did what was necessary to remove the human threat—sometimes permanently.

As usual, kill or be killed was now an everyday reality—now offensively instead of defensively. And the rats were feeling that by taking lives in this situation, albeit basically self-defense, they were saving others and preserving freedom in the South.

After all, wasn't that why they were there, to save and to preserve freedom? That's what they were told and Wergen and the rats had no time to agree, argue or doubt the freedom premise— right or wrong.

Yet this increasing lethal action was causing Wergen to become more jaded and hard-bitten yet. The tunnel activities were becoming "cut and dried;" simply search, clean out to preserve anything important, destroy the tunnel and shadow the plows or whatever tool was available for them to find the next one—allowing no one to get in their way.

But during one tunnel denial a strange thing happened to put a crack in Wergen's curing granite-hard attitude. One day the rats came upon a tunnel that at the onset appeared complex and also appeared to harbor recent activity, perhaps even at the moment, as they thought they detected human odors seeping out, yet no voices. As the routine went, with quickly summoned Cavalry reinforcements waiting close by for backup, the rats carefully maneuvered into their tunnel-entering routine on full alert with their weapons readied.

Their suspicions proved mostly correct, the activity in the tunnel had been quite recent, and quite unusual in regards to what they had been finding. When securely into the tunnel the *Rats* found a table surrounded by four stubby chairs and on the table were small saucers of rice that was still warm and cups of wine, but *no* Charlie.

The rats looked at each other registering alarm while quickly separating to form a protective stance. Was Charlie actually gone — escaping out of another entry point? Or were they still there hiding in a secret compartment of some kind waiting to pounce? Or perhaps they had just been killed atop in the jungle somewhere. *Or yet maybe they were ghosts.* An uncanny haze slowly unfolded as the rats stood frozen.

But whatever the situation they weren't there — at least in body. And if Charlie did get away only moments before, how so without noise or any trace of escape? *Maybe they were ghosts.* With the warm rice and the wine which had been very recently prepared somehow the rats felt their presence — eerie like.

As the rats left the tunnel and began to destroy it, they admitted to each other that this time they felt as though they were violating another human's property and belongings. Wergen left the denied tunnel feeling shaken and strange. They never did unravel the mystery. And Wergen has never really forgotten that day or that strange tunnel, of the hundreds he'd been involved in denying throughout his tour.

Wergen comments: I remember that tunnel well with its haunting atmosphere. It seemed charged with a supernatural shimmer that lasted throughout the tunnel far after our search had found only slight traces of Charlie's presence. That was a damn scary feeling, almost entrancing.

****

Within the next few days they were to discover another tunnel that would leave them astonished and in trouble, but not with the enemy. When they thought they had experienced all the ingenuity of Charlie's tunnel creation and uses in the Iron Triangle, they had to think again.

The tunnel they discovered had apparently been evacuated quickly when the Rome plows approached and began clearing away the foliage for the arriving rats.

When the rats were all safely in to the tunnel they shined their lights, illuminating an incredible sight. The tunnel was being used to manufacture radio controlled explosive devices — from scratch.

They found a cache of high explosives (RDX and TNT) along with stacks of sealed metal cases of Russian manufactured radio-controlled detonators, although at that moment they weren't sure what was in the cases as none of the rats were fluent in the Russian markings. But they suspected as such and, as always, they knew they had to be careful and delicate handling was the rule, regardless of what was in the cases.

The rats took a few of each type of the metal containers out of the tunnel and Wergen cautiously pried open one of them with his kbar. He stopped and sat back, seeing the first case contained the high explosive RDX; opening a second case revealed about fifty radio-controlled detonators. He quickly resealed the case, realizing the steel containers created a *Faraday Cage*, shielding away unwanted static and unwanted electrical energy.

Wergen comments: The steel case was keeping electrical energy out like a screen in the glass door of a microwave traps the microwaves inside the oven.

With a large circle of Cavalry soldiers to protect them, the rats were able to work judiciously to methodically assess what they had uncovered. They were astounded. The tunnel harbored close to

5,000 *radio controlled* detonators and approximately 1000 pounds of pure explosives. If these devices had been assembled and deployed the results could have inflicted severe damage and mayhem to the heavy concentration of American and South Vietnamese military patrolling the area.

Wergen over tunnel where enemy explosives were being assembled

The first thing the rats did was blow and tear gas the empty tunnel leaving no chance of it ever being used again. And leaving nothing to further chance, Wergen and the rats built a large pile of all the discovered explosives and detonators, moved everyone safely from the area and torched it off— creating a major, although harmless explosion.

Unfortunately, in the following days Wergen found himself in serious trouble for destroying enemy property. Appearing before the brass in an inquiry—in jeopardy of a court martial—they told him they could have probably easily discovered the frequency and then have pre-triggered any devices wherever they might be…or whatever.

Wergen weakly agreed, yet insisted that although his action might have been hasty, no U.S. soldier or civilian was harmed by such a massive storm of explosives that *could have* ended up loose in the hands of the enemy; finally, now there would be no booby traps waiting for targets of opportunity. At end, when cooler heads prevailed Wergen was left alone with only a warning—not forgotten—but left alone.

Wergen comments: Besides protecting the military, another reason I decided to blow the cache up is because I had a military friend in Saigon that kept track of captured enemy weapons, such as serial numbers, country

of manufacture, etc.; and that he suspected many captured weapons turned back up on the battlefield in the south – in enemy hands.

Obviously if this was true, this was done through some corrupt connections in the U.S. ranks. I understood that all captured weapons were supposed to be sent to Taiwan to arm and train their army but somehow they didn't always get there as they were probably detoured into Haiphong Harbor. Anyway, I wasn't taking any chances that any weapon like this would ever be used against me.

****

One of their last days before the rats were to head back to their home base in Di-An, began normal enough considering the unusual experiences they had come across since they arrived in the Iron triangle. Yet it would hardly end up that way. Wergen went ahead of his rat team and felt tranquil riding on an APC leaning against its turret while trailing a few yards behind a D-9 dozer. They were all looking for tunnel action.

He felt good with another day closer to home, although he was still morose over thinking about spending the upcoming Thanksgiving holidays alone and away from his family. He nonchalantly tipped his steel helmet forward and closed his eyes, when he suddenly heard a loud warning cry "look out" from the APC driver.

Wergen jerked forward, focusing ahead as he frantically looked for what and where the danger was. He spotted it! Just to their left the dozer was pushing a big pile of foliage and rolling in front, wobbling like a fumbled football, was a US 500 pound unexploded bomb the dozer had unearthed. There was no time to defensively react. Wergen's world became really loud with that dreaded KFB action, while a fragment hit him in the head, knocking him off the APC.

The explosion blew the 5-ton c-frame clean off the dozer along with the driver. Wergen remembers later lying on the ground next to the APC with a medic tending to him before moving him to rest in the shade. Refusing to go back to a bunker, he spent the rest of the day denying tunnels while nursing, in Wergen's words: *"one hell of a headache."*

****

Days afterward Wergen and his rats felt happy as they sat in the chopper heading back to their home base in Di-An to rest during the holiday, and perhaps to finally get a decent break before their next duty assignment. But if they had known what lay just ahead they may have requested to stay in the Iron Triangle denying tunnels. The future held another graduating step in Wergen's deadly warfare action.

Chapter Nine

Di-An — Base Camp, 1st Infantry Division — Southwest Bien Hoa

The rain had been persistent but finally diminished leaving a humid pall over Di-An. Sergeant Thomas E. Wergen wearing damp jungle fatigues, donned by a flak vest, sat on a gun-jeep hood picking away at his Thanksgiving Dinner — cold turkey loaf out of a C-ration can. He felt somber and uncomfortable. He had just heard that Hanoi had outwardly rejected President Johnson's latest peace gesture. The war would press on.

Wergen holding thanksgiving "c" ration turkey loaf. Notice catch-hook at left to snap piano wire on roads to prevent beheading

But he was here on base and out of direct combat for the time being. After all, that was more than enough to be thankful for today, he decided while looking for any self-consolation. But that didn't really work. He had just learned one of his closest army buddies, Lawrence Stapleton, who he'd met at the Army chemical school in Alabama, and then traveled with to teach at the infantry school at Fort Benning, GA, hadn't made it through the week. His chopper went down while on a *snoopy* mission.

Wergen comments: Only two beings on earth give off ammonia when they perspire, humans and monkeys. The army had a squadron of Huey choppers each fitted with an ammonia sniffer and dubbed them "snoopy."

Most of the chemical corps soldiers sent to Viet Nam was assigned duty to one of these snoops' to operate and read the complicated registering equipment while in flight. I found my capacity in tunnel denial and was spared this highly hazardous duty.

The snoopy choppers were required to fly at a low altitude of roughly 150 feet and at a sluggish speed of about 100 knots to enable efficient "sniffing" of the thick jungle for concentrations of ammonia. When they detected a suspicious area they would radio the position quadrants and then either the U.S. heavy artillery or allied fighter aircraft would respond, hammering the area to hopefully quash more than monkeys.

Overall this was an effective military operation, except these lumbering "snoopy missions" provided easy targets for enemy ground fire. Just like everything else the U.S. threw at the North, it didn't take them long to learn how to return combat in turn. Snoopy crashes and casualties were common and many of them involved Wergen's friends he had met in the line of duty and chemical army training.

Wergen comments: I wrote to Larry Stapleton's parents after I learned he was killed. Although it was extremely difficult I felt as his best Army buddy they needed to hear from me.

They sent me a Christmas card thanking me and wishing me well. I thought that was really nice of them to take the time, and made me feel good about having contacted them.

As usual, Wergen wondered what the day held in store for him. He was briefed that he and his rats were going to inspect and search for tunnels within the expansive cemetery located just outside of Di-An base camp as there was intermittent sniper action coming from just inside the perimeter. They hadn't lost anyone yet, but that cost was only a matter of time if the episodes were allowed to continue. And of course the belligerent incidents were quite exasperating and unnerving—most probably the main intent of the shooter.

At first Wergen thought that any necessary desecration of graves even while searching for enemy tunnels was taboo even under the rules of warfare.

But then Wergen was told of the Viet Nam funeral culture: when a Vietnamese dies the burial procession is quite ceremonious on the way to the cemetery; and once at graveside, paying the respects is major yet a one-time event. It's unusual for friends and family members to ever return. Instead, every year they honor their departed loved ones at their home with incense, offerings of food, money and flowers to each other as in a "Day of the Dead" celebration.

Di-An Cemetery adjacent to Home-Base – hiding tunnels and snipers

Therefore, Charlie would take advantage of that cultured belief of grave absence, certainly in an area where it would prove advantageous to their combat tactics. They would simply observe an current ritual or search the cemetery for a fresh grave, then deepen and interconnect the adjoining gravesites creating a new complex tunnel system. The entrance was usually fabricated under the grave marker. Consequently, the cemetery adjacent to the U.S. military base would be a strategic place for grave-tunnels to house a brazen Charlie.

Wergen comments: A cemetery sniper wasn't common, especially right outside the base. But it happened. A few times they ended up "digging their own graves," so to speak.

Still, Wergen shook his head thinking that destruction of gravesites for any reason might still be pushing the envelope, as he flipped the empty c-can into the trash barrel.

Yet regardless of what he thought, he knew this unusual investigation would have to be carried out just like every new slice of nasty warfare he was having to experience. He knew that well. He hopped off the jeep and went to find his fellow rats. Yeah, right, he thought with a sneer, while still mourning inwardly over losing his close friend, Lawrence…Happy Thanksgiving.

Wergen's Thanksgiving Day would become more frustrating yet as he and his rats were sent to the cemetery to search diligently yet carefully, while still considering the hallowed site. They found a few shallow abandoned tunnels, yet *no* Charlie or any suspected site that might be housing the sniper.

Wergen comments: We went again to search on several occasions in the following days, to no avail. Yet the sniper must have felt the pressure as the shooting eventually stopped.

****

Sergeant Wergen and his rats had not gone unnoticed while denying hundreds of tunnels in different regions of Viet Nam. By the end of 1967 their fierce and lethal military reputation was strongly established — especially the effectiveness of their search and demolition strategies. Thus they began receiving unusual calls from unusual places.

In early December, Sgt. Wergen was to go through another major combat transition. He thought that his current Viet Nam realm was perilous enough, but he was to experience another extreme level of hazardous warfare. He'd be joining missions with the elements of service he'd only heard about when soldiers got careless and talked out of hand; those being the vaguest of secret missions with the 5th group 1st Special Forces. Being summoned by this unit was the beginning of the rat's covert operations and the further enhancement of their standings as full combat soldiers. They would end up earning those reputations as they would go on *highly secret* missions, usually across the border into the *most hostile* of enemy territory.

And they would even be called upon to join several select missions headed by the heralded MACV-SOG division. Because they only went on a few select SOG missions they had no time to train, or bedrock their positions with that unit.

Wergen comments: The majority of our missions were with the 5th group 1st Special Forces so none of us rats had any solid idea what MACV-SOG was and had never really asked about how you got into it, practicing the golden rule in the military: speak only when spoken to.

Yet we soon realized this branch was unquestionably professional and made up of the most competent hand-picked fighters. Later I learned that selected SOG individuals from all of the military divisions went through a few weeks of intense physical and mental training which was actually conducted in Viet Nam. I'd also learned that many top notch soldiers from the 101st Airborne and from the Army Rangers failed to meet the grade.

We probably would have also failed the training, but our schooling was only one day – report secretly to your group and head out on a mission. That was our total SOG training – live and real combat.

Officially Declassified Military Clarification: MACV-SOG (Military Assistance Command, Vietnam - Studies and observation Group) had five primary responsibilities with the capability and authorization to undertake additional special missions as required. Primary responsibilities included: (1) *Cross-border operations* regularly conducted to disrupt the VC, Khmer Rouge, Pathet Lao and the NVA in their own territories; (2) Keeping track of all imprisoned and missing Americans and *conducting raids* to assist and free them as part of the Escape and Evasion (E & E) mission definition for all captured U.S. personnel and downed airmen; (3) Training and *dispatching agents* into North Vietnam to help and actually operate resistance movement operations; (4) Conduct "Black" psychological operations, such as establishing false (national) NVA broadcasting stations inside North Vietnam; (5) Conduct "Gray" psychological operations as typified by the Hue-Phu-Bai propaganda transmitter. MACV-SOG was also assigned with specific tasks such as kidnapping and covert insertion of rigged ammo into the enemy ammunition supply system, which were designed to explode and destroy their crews upon use. MACV-SOG was often sent for retrieval of sensitive documents and equipment if lost or captured through enemy action. They executed in any way necessary based on their discretion and utmost secrecy.

Further Unofficial Military Clarification: During Vietnam conceivably no group of men has created more interest or exhibited more heroism than the Soldiers, Marines, Sailors and Airmen of the MACV-SOG service. Operating in top secrecy and far away from the support of the vast military machine, they were the eyes, ears and the tip of the sword.

****

In early December when Wergen and his rats were initially called to the 5th Group 1st Special Forces their main mission objectives were to intercept and interdict enemy supply convoys. They were now on the war offensive. They spent weeks of elapsed time mapping and mining the Ho Chi Minh Trail (heavily and naturally obscured by jungle growth and prolific gnarled tree covering) to blow up convoys, *or* just watching and calculating where the supplies originated—not always necessarily from the North. The rats would then accumulate and report strategic information as to when, and mainly what route the convoys were coming from, so the U.S. could attack them with heavy artillery or air power. It was an ongoing and grinding undertaking.

In the early sixties substantial construction of the Ho Chi Minh trail had actually began at the North Vietnam coast to support the southern movement of troops and supplies. The trail gradually developed into a 1500 mile web of dense jungle and mountain passes extending along Vietnam's western border through Laos and parts of Cambodia.

Since then the trail funneled a constant stream of northern soldiers and supplies into the highlands of South Vietnam. At first stage, the slogging journey took about six months to complete. By 1968 the trek will take only six weeks due to road improvements by North Vietnamese laborers, many of whom are women.

The first U.S. air strikes were ordered against the Ho Chi Minh trail in late 1965. Throughout the war, the trail is continually bombed by American jets with little success in halting the tremendous flow of soldiers and supplies from the North. Approximately 500 American fighter jets will be lost attacking the trail. After each attack, bomb damage along the trail is swiftly repaired, again mainly by female construction crews.

Wergen and the rats felt somewhat fortunate with this dangerous, but less-hazardous duty of impeding enemy movement along the Ho Chi Minh trail, considering the missions other groups of the Special Forces were being assigned to; however, their so-called fortune was short-lived. They were soon summoned to join other type of missions comprised of high secrecy; heavy jungle trudges; and many times waged direct combat against an enemy that usually significantly outnumbered them.

Wergen com,ments: Our overall vision of this phase of our war was kept narrow and unclear. The less we knew about the exact objective, the better, and perhaps safer should we be captured. We were assigned to a group, promptly given a rough objective outline, and told to follow along until we were to do our part.

I'll always remember the first time a Special Forces officer taught us how to walk silently and "invisibly" through the jungle: Stride on the balls of your feet and not heel to toe; constantly watching where you're going, as a piece of dry bamboo sounds like a gunshot... if you step on it.

We also had to be alert for the flora and fauna or "wait-a-minute" vines. They're covered with needle-like thorns and these climbers grew up, down, and across the common foliage. And once you're caught up in them, it was almost impossible to escape. At the least, struggling free was quite noisy. On one mission we were ambushed, and I got caught up in one. I was helpless at the moment so I pretended I was dead and prayed. That's the only time the vines came in handy for me.

And they taught us how to be vigilant not to brush against bushes or tree limbs, not only for the noise issue, but you had to be careful not to break the branches so you might be easily followed by people who wanted to end your life.

And there was a nasty little poisonous snake called a krait that was sort of meek. But you definitely didn't want to unknowingly disturb them at night when they were on the go; or when they were lying in wait for their rodent dinner in piles of leaves or grasses. They were so small their bite was unnoticeable. We had a mercenary once who was bitten while lying down in the jungle and he was dead by morning. It took the medics hours to figure it out. He had been bitten on the ear.

The careful traipsing of Special Force squads included watching for the natural perils of poisonous reptiles, wild animals and of course, booby traps—but there was worse dread. The enemy knew they'd be coming sooner or later. They just didn't know precisely when and exactly where. Therefore the intensity of these missions was all day and all night. No one could relax for even one minute, as *that* minute they let their guard down opened the potential to get them killed, and perhaps everyone else in the group.

Wergen comments: I remember a sergeant in charge bellowed on leaving for a mission, 'Don't speak until asked for a reply and then mouth it wordlessly, or use hand-signals, if possible.' During many of the missions we wouldn't talk or even breathe which might utter any sound whatsoever. Their special mission jungle war edict: follow orders; keep your mouth shut; learn what you can as fast as you can; keep your eyes open and your powder dry, and perhaps you'll stay alive.

If they didn't feel you could follow that creed, you didn't go…actually you were probably never picked in the first place.

****

Just before Christmas 1967, Wergen and the rats were called on to join one of the more involved missions to flush out and ambush an expected key supply convoy traveling along the Ho Chi Minh trail close to the Cambodian border. The undertaking was quite involved and highly covert, so the rats had teamed up with an experienced Special Forces Hatchet Squad out of Kontum—including some mercenary Cambodians. They needed to find an area of the trail suitable for a straightforward attack on the convoy, along with completing the mapping for future attacks—striving to shut that section of the route down altogether. The jaunt would begin routinely but soon fell chaotic and slowly deteriorated when they ran into major resistance—with the situation never improving.

They knew this mission would be extremely difficult because the estimated target-area of the trail was covered by triple-canopy jungle making it extremely difficult to navigate, as no stars were ever visible at night, and during the day only a slight beam of sunlight filtered through the leaves. Visibility would naturally wane to a few meters—in fact, any contact with the enemy in this type of jungle averaged 3- to 15-meters at best.

Wergen comments: This limited visibility was an element we faced often during these missions. But this is usually the setting while on covert warfare jungle operations…not really surprising.

The morning began as scheduled with the slicks arriving on time at Di-An to pick them up and ferry them to a safe and purportedly secure landing zone (LZ) within their objective area, although knowingly peppered with enemy. Everything appeared to be going as planned until they had all landed and started to exit the slicks. Then all hell broke loose! They were being ambushed by enemy "watchers!"

Wergen comments: Charlie was tenacious and patient at assigning a few troops to watch and observe potential jungle LZ's. Unfortunately this one was not only being "watched" but it appeared that a company of the NVA had stopped to rest close to the area, which wasn't unusual considering the hostile region. And they were quickly advancing to join the attack.

Dodging enemy fire from both sides of the oval shaped LZ, The group, including Wergen and his rats, raced to dive for cover in the heavy undergrowth.

They were being attacked assuredly by an over-manned enemy!

The slicks swiftly began to evacuate while the door gunners not only inflicted enemy casualties, but mainly provided some relief at keeping Charlie pinned down with their sporadic fire while the squad hunkered down in the thick foliage.

The frustration mounted as Wergen and the group were not prepared for a sustained firefight and the C&C (command and communications) slick radioed they were going to have to get out of there fast, as they were becoming easy targets from the escalating enemy rocket fire coming from the jungle.

Shouting through the continuous cracking of gunfire, the radioman frantically requested an ammo drop from *somewhere* but was quickly told there was none to drop; the slicks were "taxis," not war-supply units.

Wergen comments: Understandably there was no real help there. In fact, even our simple radio was inferior...only good for about fifteen miles so the messages were being relayed through an airborne partner and fading fast.

The LZ and surrounding proximity was supposed to have been reasonably secured and basically undetectable; but that critical judgment-error mattered little now. They were in a fire fight for their lives! It was a live or die scenario as being captured was *not* a sane option!

Wergen comments: We were spread out, holding our own while shooting carefully and sparingly, as we didn't have an abundant supply of ammo. But we believed we had our positions secure. There was a lot of dead enemy, compared to our losses.

A couple of guys from our squad had captured and dragged one of the the NVA who had been shot in the chest. He had a sucking chest wound and obviously wasn't long for life. But he was still uncooperative when it came to answering questions about how many of the enemy was out there...and where.

The squad needed answers fast! Fortunately, they had a ruthless Cambodian medic/interpreter and after about the third time he asked the wounded NVA soldier without getting answers, he stuck his finger in the bullet hole and wiggled it around.

Wergen comments: One could only in their wildest nightmare imagine the pain of that. The wounded guy screamed and started talking. We found out they were replacements for an NVA unit to the west and were resting before heading out again. That's all we learned because either the pain or blood loss...or both had killed him. But the info was enough!

Of course, it was now too late to continue their mission, as their position was compromised so they radioed for exit orders. The original slicks were out of fuel and ammo and not planning or able to re-enter that enemy-laden LZ. The group was instructed to fight their way to an area approximately two kilometers away to meet up with incoming choppers to pick them up. Fortunately it was to their south so they wouldn't have to go through the enemy to get there — they were north.

Wergen and the group spent the next two hours running and fighting while taking their wounded with them to the new evacuation area. They were careful not to take a direct route so as to leave that for a last-minute dash because the incoming choppers may not be able to land in an overly hostile LZ.

Wergen comments: Just as we were making our last sprint to the LZ and the waiting choppers, with some gunships overhead providing cover, the enemy pursuit and shooting had slowed.

But then we passed another LP (listening post) with a couple of persistent Charlie dashing out for a fight. One of the Cambodians in our group shot one in the chest with an M-79 grenade launcher, separating his head clean off from his body. This seemed quite amusing to the shooter as he wouldn't stop smiling while he jumped into the chopper; he was probably entertained at how fast the other seemed to have disappeared out of fright that another round was coming his way.

We took our badly wounded and got out of that one all right; but the bad news is we were going to have to go back again. And I had been hit. Fortunately it was a minor wound, but the bullet was still in my backside. A Merry Christmas greeting, from Charlie!

On the journey back to friendly territory while the medics were tending to the more severely wounded, Wergen squeezed out the bullet, like a teenager popping a pimple, and stuffed the wound with some bandage material he found lying on the deck.

Wergen comments: Bullets are hot and they're painful. So my extraction effort provided instant relief. The medics were busy anyway.

Unfortunately, however, the wound was deep enough to become infected as it took Wergen several days to get back to Di-An. When the base doctor took one look at the serious festering in Wergen's backside, he immediately sent him to the hospital.

Wergen comments: I remember the hospital in Long Binh at Christmas in 1967. It was a horrible experience with casualties overflowing into the passageways...screams of death and bellowing of STAT! STAT! every few minutes. Stat is doctor jargon for right now! I remember the place was a huge interconnected maze of tents and wooden slats for sidewalks. All in all, that experiece was absolutely horrifying.

Wergen's injury wasn't as minor as he had thought. They had him do sits' baths numerous times a day — that is, applying scalding hot water to the wound and hope it satisfactorily drew out the poisons. When Wergen's injury finally began to heal, he was told he had to plan on a few more days of observation because if the infection had spread it might prove hazardous to his internal organs.

Wergen was despondent over having to spend more time in the hospital. But on Christmas Eve when Dunning and Cowboy came to visit him, they all decided this was not a fun place to spend the holiday. They helped him "escape" the hospital, and the next day they found some wine and cooked turkey back at their home base.

Wergen and the rats weren't pleased about how they had to spend Christmas, along with a couple of lazy days afterward in this hell-hole. But they, along with rest of the U.S. Military, had no idea of what they were about to face in the most bloodstained phase of the Viet Nam war — the new year of 1968, and TET.

Chapter Ten
The Turning-Point Year — Early January 1968 — Di-An

There was substantial concern filling the steamy air as the old year rolled into 1968. Overall, the conflict in South Vietnam stubbornly remained basically unchanged. Yet the South Vietnamese Armed Forces (ARVN) *was* becoming more proactive and militarily capable under U.S. leadership. They assumed increased responsibility for manning and gradually heading up several Special Forces camps and the many CIDG companies throughout the South.

Wergen comments: The CIDG — Civilian Irregular Defense Group — strategy was developed around 1962 when U.S. Special Forces traveled to areas that were under minimal control of the South. The Special Forces' main purpose was to provide para-military training to the locals who wanted to protect their independence from the North.

They began the training with the Montagnards ("people from the mountains") in the Central Highlands. This strategy was proving so effective they spread the training to other areas in the South over the next few years — building up to actual separate CIDG camps (companies).

The first CIDG companies were mainly "border-watchers" tracking and reporting on suspected enemy movement from the North. But eventually they developed into regular armed troops for the South and were placed into Special Forces' camps. They went on missions with the South Vietnamese Forces as advisors — proving extremely valuable.

As 1968 began the military bases were becoming more solid with the South Vietnamese Army thus the U.S. advisors would relinquish leadership command and trickle out. The development of this increased responsibility among the South created a U.S. *desired* "sense of confidence and optimism." In unison, the South forces being equally enthusiastic, responded by conducting further major offensive operations that had increased at the end of 1967.

Yet U.S. military anxiety remained thick sensing that the heaviest fighting still lay ahead. Despite the success of the U.S. and South Vietnamese Army beefed up operations, there were acute signals in the fall of 1967 that pointed to an aggressive enemy build-up—surrounding the South—specifically in proximity to Laos and Cambodia.

Also in the fall the northern forces had brazenly attacked the Special Forces camps of Loc Ninh and Dak To, close to where the borders of Laos, Cambodia and South Vietnam meet.

In response, U.S. military troop strength in Vietnam was growing to more than 500,000, reinforcing these regions of main concern with battalions of men and military might. In addition, there were 61,000 allied troops and 600,000 South Vietnamese complementing the U.S. forces. This period would prove to employ the heaviest troop participation in any span of the war.

Tunnel rat, Sergeant Thomas Wergen, was firmly in the midst of it. The blues of being homesick and missing the 1967 holidays had worn off and he was back in his "staying alive" mode. He just wanted to move on and pass the days.

Entering his second calendar-year in Viet Nam, Wergen was doing what was asked of him and sometimes more. His war life of tunnel denial, grabbing sleep anywhere and anytime, usually waking in an exhausted haze, finding himself being shot at during running gun battles was back in full force—and again, a basic existence to him.

In addition to this he was also getting called on to participate in short covert missions, dubbed "Sneaky Petes" with the 5th group 1st Special Forces. Yet he was only trying to stay calm and in control, while moving another day closer for home. He was here and would strive to complete his duty in exemplary fashion, but he was no war hawk at heart.

Meanwhile, despite the ongoing success of the obvious U.S. and the South Vietnamese Army overpowering operations, there were stronger indications in the beginning days of 1968 that *still more* of an enemy build-up was occurring, particularly in those already threatened areas close to Laos and Cambodia. Yet the enemy offensive operations had dropped off significantly. They had stopped attacking. The war zone was strangely quiet.

This stillness was one of the main reasons the scuttlebutt and hearsay of an oncoming onslaught by the North (later dubbed *the TET offensive*) began to filter in as early as December. Yet nothing lay definite in the forward eyes of the U.S. and the South, only intelligence reports written by the U.S. Army's *Psychological Operations* department (PYSOPS) located in Saigon. Yet these reports bore credence as this department specialized in studying the minds and hearts of the enemy. This was their job—human nature, war psychology and typewriters—not guns.

Wergen comments: I had a friend, Harry N. Snelling, a Specialist 5 intelligence analyst with the 4th Psychological Operations group. They had a formal job description, but basically their responsibility was to screw around with the hearts and minds of the enemy. He was a busy man at this time...they all were.

The fortified compound of the U.S. Army's psychological Operations Dept (PSYOPS) in Saigon

The first official report out of PSYOPS predicted that a major assault was probable to occur soon, most likely on Christmas, but certainly if not Christmas then on TET in late January, as this would be an ideal time for the enemy to utilize their covert tactics. PYSOPS reasoned among the other aforementioned signs, TET is a Vietnamese holiday in which all the Vietnamese desperately strive to be back in their home towns, villages or hamlets, to be with their families. Several thousand ARVN soldiers were even known and expected to go AWOL to be with their families during TET.

Additionally, the holiday mass exodus of civilians clogging the roads and paths; would be a perfect shield for the VC and the NVA infiltrators to skulk among the people, selecting their prime target areas. The report also stated the pragmatic premise that the enemy would move through and use the tunnels to their advantage.

Yet any reports that the North was strategically planning to attack military bases and cause upheaval throughout the South remained at its height, only a solid possibility, calling for added caution. Unknowingly then, of course, this *possibility* would turn into a grim, harsh reality for the U.S. and its allies, striking on Tet, January 31, 1968—Vietnam's New Year's Day.

Harry N. Snelling, Specialist 5 comments: I was involved in some of the reports for PYSOPS. No one is exactly sure why the TET offensive was such a pronounced surprise to key military personnel. Perhaps they didn't read the informational intelligent reports we wrote...or they didn't hold these reports keenly relevant to the jungle reality of the tapered enemy offense.

They may have reasoned the recent decline in enemy activity was not due to the North's strategy at prioritizing the building up forces for an aggressive attack, but instead due to the U.S. and the South's aggressive operations that were decimating the enemy forces – thereby increasing that U.S. desired "sense of confidence and optimism."

Specialist Harry Snelling and the PSYOPS department he worked for should and would know what they were talking about when it came to predicted war strategy of the enemy. Although typewriters were the main tool of the PSYOPS specialists, they would don weapons and face combat reality a significant amount of their time while performing their job. They would be assigned a war mission that would begin in the battlefield for a few weeks and then return to Saigon and their office to write up an in-depth report and an anticipated warfare briefing on their findings.

Besides that PSYOPS would also operate leaflet drop missions over the South, attempting to destroy the will of the VC and NVA and to stop their fighting. They would dump boxes and boxes of propaganda documents (flyers) and hope some of the messages would take hold.

Harry Snelling comments: I would volunteer to fly on these missions on weekends. After flying ten missions, you would be awarded an Air Combat Crew member's Badge. I felt those wings would look cool on my uniform. After twenty missions, an Air Medal would be awarded. I thought that would be an added really cool uniform bonus. Well…at first anyway.

Specialist Snelling was on his seventh or eighth mission flying in a C-47 (DC-3 Gooney Bird) of the Second World War vintage. Among other acclaims they were the planes that "flew the hump" over the Himalayas to deliver supplies to China. For purposes of dropping the leaflets a large square hole had been cut into the deck of the fuselage through which the boxes of leaflets were dumped.

Snelling comments: Sometimes if we were circling we could see the VC picking the flyers up and waving them across their butt, indicating what they intended to use the flyers for. We weren't deterred. We felt that if one VC stopped killing because of the flyers then the boxes, time and effort was worth the saving of even one life. So we kept it up.

Snelling remembers a leaflet drop mission in early January. They were flying over an area that had been hit by American B-52 bombers. Relaxed and marveling at how the area looked like a moonscape, Snelling dumped the last box of leaflets through the deck and sat back. He anticipated a short flight back to Bien Hoa Airbase and looked forward to being closer to receiving that *Air Combat Crew member's Badge*. But it was not to be.

The pilot began an abrupt descent until they could effectively use the giant loudspeakers the plane was equipped with. The aggressive crew chief had changed plans and had turned on a tape recorder that began broadcasting Vietnamese propaganda messages through the speakers while Snelling looked on nervously through the porthole.

Snelling comments: Well, after a few minutes these snapping, buzzing things came flinging through the deck of the fuselage. They were like angry hornets. Lead hornets. The damn VC were shooting at us and we were broadcasting our position…in their language, yet. Of course we ducked and bobbed around. Now I'm 6'5" and made a pretty good target…but fortunately no one was hit.

Suddenly there was a loud noise to the right as Snelling looked out just in time to see the starboard engine flame out—only the second engine was keeping them aloft. The plane keeled left but the pilot managed to straighten it out and hold level flight. The pilot then made a long and slow wide turn, heading back to Bien Hoa. After a few minutes the crew chief stepped from the cockpit looking ashen as he hurried aft through the cabin.

Snelling comments: Of course I knew there was nothing good about our situation, except the shooting had stopped. There were two E4's with my team from PSYOPS. The crew chief wanted us to jump because the pilot wasn't sure he could maintain a safe altitude, even though he was desperately trying to get the plane back to Bien Hoa.

We all quickly agreed that we felt safer in the plane than jumping into "wherever," therefore we all refused to jump even under the threat of disobeying the pilot's order. But we knew that was an unlawful order. We held fast. I believe the pilot thought the lighter weight with us gone would give him a better chance of making Bien Hoa, but I don't know that for sure.

The crew chief shook his head in frustration and returned to the cockpit. He remained in the cockpit until the plane wobbled onto the final approach for Bien Hoa. The pilot announced for us to fasten our seat belts and to prepare for a bumpy landing as the crew chief joined us to honker down in the cabin, while remaining sheepish and silent. The plane hit hard and landed crazily under emergency alert, but the pilot was able to bring it down in one piece with no injuries.

Snelling comments: After we were on the ground, the pilot and co-pilot wouldn't even leave the cockpit until we were off, and away from the aircraft. We had our M16's with us. I think they were a little afraid of us and what they had asked us to do over hostile no-man's land.

When I returned to Saigon and reported what had happened, my commanding officer asked me to join him for a private chat. He had me go over the detail twice. I'm not sure of his motive, but he ordered me to not do any more leaflet drop missions – period. He was probably concerned about the two E4's that were following my lead in the plane and didn't jump. So, no cool Air Medals and no wings. But I'm not sure I cared about never riding in one of those planes again.

✼✼✼✼✼✼✼✼✼✼✼✼

In early January SOG called on Sgt. Wergen (the rest of the rats were spread out on other minor assignments) to join a small group of roughly twelve of their fighters. Their operation was planned as a short mission, basically to be gone only overnight, just across the Laos border. The objective was to plant listening devices near a strategic portion of the Ho Chi Minh Trail for gathering U.S. intelligence that would aid the blitzing of enemy supply convoys. And the U.S. powers also thought these devices might provide additional data to support the determination of any TET offensive facts, which were still only cautionary reports.

A key element of this mission was to avoid any contact with the enemy — get in, plant the devices and get out fast! No enemy firefights unless absolutely necessary to stay alive. The thought was that these planted devices were to be a keen investigative tool and the enemy was not to be tipped off that any one from the South was even in the area. Otherwise they'd surely begin a search and set plans to protect the region while clearing any intrusions they might find.

As bad luck would have it however, the group spotted an NVA battalion off in the distance when they were trekking silently to the main planting target from the LZ. The SOG group immediately hunkered down and froze in the jungle cover, setting their evasive maneuver in motion. Remembering their key order to dodge the enemy, they were to quickly move out of there without noise, without casualties and without arousing any suspicion. They could then regroup at a safe location and come back to try again.

Regardless, they all knew this mission was too critical to scratch, certainly important enough for no rush to failure. There was time for them to think it through. At the moment, they all knew the drill: carefully retreat, and no-talking. Just follow the basic stealthy conduct and communicate with each other using only slight hand signals, if at all even necessary.

They were safely moving away from the unsuspecting NVA battalion when more bad luck struck again. Beginning to pick up their pace, they were moving silently through the jungle when suddenly the point man stopped abruptly and raised his hand, pointing upward. They all froze!

Wergen and the rest looked up in dread at seeing a large Vietnamese tiger lying on a tree limb above the trail, peering down at them. They all immediately realized the rub. As there were no other war noises in the area — especially gunshots — if any one of them were to recklessly shoot the tiger, the NVA, outnumbering them roughly thirty to one, would certainly grasp their position and perhaps then able to hunt them down. Or if one, or a few of the squad were to pull their knives and go hand to paw with the animal — the noise of snarling and screeching would certainly produce the same feared enemy results.

Even though the cat was smaller than a Bengal, it was still large with sharp claws, long teeth and quick afoot; therefore, the size was no real consolation. And of course it lay superior in its part of the world. For a few horrible seconds they all looked at each other, and then turned to the point man. He shrugged a no-choice and slowly signaled to draw their knives, while motioning to proceed forward.

Perspiring profusely in the hot and humid afternoon heat, they began their careful exit looking at where they placed each footstep so as not to make any noise in their edgy state. While making this effort, each had to keep a nervous eye on the cat, and, of course, behind them for any approaching enemy.

Their luck turned as the cat — most likely not hungry — just lay there on the limb and watched them all go by, without any one of them or the cat uttering a sound until the squad was finally safely out of the area. The group found a spot and settled down for a rest and released sighs of relief before deciding their next move.

Wergen comments: We all sat there saying nothing with our heads hung, surely thanking whatever gods we worshipped that the cat wasn't interested in playing, or having any of us for dinner.

This was damn scary battlefield terror. Maybe not actual blood and gore but all of our lives may have hinged on the impulse and unknown behavior of that wild animal.

We may be the best fighting mililary in the world...the best equipped...the best trained, yet perhaps we end up dying over something we had no control of whatsoever. No control other than a dozen men doing their best to avoid confrontation with man and a beast while silently escaping the situation. We had made it again – so far, anyway.

The squad decided to radio for a LZ pickup and return in a few days. They just didn't trust their luck and wits any more today.

Chapter Eleven
"Mike Force" Assassins — Tet Counteroffensive — January 1968

The day was growing staid and murky as Sgt. Wergen sat back in his empty hooch finishing a cold beer while reliving the stress from that Laos SOG mission of a few days ago. He shook his head, thinking about his brush with death and how lucky they were to escape disaster with the tiger and THE NVA battalion they had unintentionally stumbled upon.

Another chapter of Wergen's war had made him realize how vulnerable he was — hardly bullet proof. He had experienced more tangled perilous moments, any of which could have snuffed out his life. Yet as usual, he had convinced himself to restore his faith and give in to his own mortality. If not, he would be lost as an effective weapon, no longer of any value to himself or the war system, regardless if the conflict may be flawed.

He *would* make it another six months. He had no choice. If he didn't rationalize his existence here, he might end up totally strained like the Special Forces guy he witnessed flipping out until he had to be tranquilized with a dart gun, strapped between two stretchers and sent on his way to Japan for the rubber-room treatment. This was not a route he wanted to take.

Wergen gazed upward, feeling pleased that the second Laos mission had gone well and with the squad finally undetected were able to plant some devices, albeit not where they wanted; yet better than not at all. He hoped their effort would shed some light on the enemy's movements and especially add any intelligence to the increasing concern and rampant rumors about a predicted widespread TET offensive.

The situation was puzzling and highly suspicious that Charlie hadn't voided the Christmas cease fire and attacked then — as most of the U.S. powers had anticipated — while the Americans were wrapped up in their "tears of happiness and joy." He smirked over the happiness and tears thought, but grew solemn again thinking how strange there was reportedly no real response coming anywhere from the North right now.

Wergen comments: It was odd all right. I remember hearing one officer at mess earlier that morning telling a large group at the table how they can't get any serious response from the North, no matter how hard we were trying to "pick fights." He suspected something was up – big time. I didn't pay much attention to his concern though. I saw no point in it, because it was still all war...we were committed until we rotated out or "until death do us part."

Wergen clowns with *Rat*, Sgt. Dunning during "down time"

Wergen finished his beer and stood while wondering about the new assignment he and Pvt. Dunning would begin tomorrow with a large group of Asian mercenaries attached to the "Mike Force." He wondered how difficult it would be to train them in demolition tactics of emplacing hundreds of land mines and setting booby traps in preparation for a major mission across the border into Cambodia. Unfortunately, the majority of them couldn't speak English.

Wergen comments: The communication issue with these guys really worried me. Maybe I was scared like never before. And this time it had little to do with exact contact with the enemy. There would be a lot of them who had never been around explosives and they couldn't speak English.

Yet perhaps the worst part of this operation for Wergen was going to *Camp Dunard* for the mission training. The motley base, located in the Southeast corner of Phuoc Long Province, was once a French fort that had been abandoned after their defeat in 1954 by the North. The base boundaries formed triangular in shape with a small area sectioned off inside for the Americans chiefly consisting of a bunk-hooch, communication shack and mess hall. The outside perimeter was reinforced with barbed wire and an outlying field was peppered with claymore's to keep Charlie out and the allied troops inside somewhat secure. The main camp also had hooches for about 200 indigenous troops and room for a few vehicles — more wire and more mines shielded any unoccupied areas.

Between the main camp entrance and the Cambodian border was a coarse airstrip capable of handling C-123 and C-130 military transport planes loaded with food, supplies and ammunition; however, it was rarely safe for the planes to land there. And most always they wouldn't.

South Vietnamese Special Force camp "Dunard" with Mike Force Mercenaries – Notice two-word slogan on building roof at center right

The planes would fly over and parachute the goods off the back-loading ramp. If there was any mail, the co-pilot would throw the mail bag out the window while aiming and hoping to miss the propellers.

Wergen comments: Dunard was a real swell place, all right. It was a treacherous area close to the western border. And you never knew who was really in there. And you never wanted to walk around there unarmed or alone, or you might get killed in your own base camp...real swell.

The transports like the 123's were our main source of supplies... food, bullets and sometimes beer if it could withstand the "delivery." The planes would be traveling about 100 mph and they'd lower the back ramps and pop the chutes...and out would come all our containers. Inevitably one or more of the pallets would catch a corner of the plane and our stuff would end up all over the jungle. Then it was a race between our guys and Charlie to see who reached the goods first.

Once when I was there our mail bag was shredded by a propeller. So a bunch of us radioed up that if it happened again we were going to start

shooting at them when they flew by. That confetti-mail event didn't happen anymore. The crew chiefs started throwing the mailbags out the side door...behind the propellers.

On one occasion we had a radio but couldn't reach anybody because it had a short range. So one day a couple of the engineers cut down a tall bamboo tree for a mast; and then we jacked up a jeep and took the wheel off the rim and using barbed wire as guy wires, we wrapped the wire around the wheel, started the jeep and raised the new radio mast. The radio operator got into some trouble that night as he got on and pitched, "This is radio free Dunard, does anyone hear me." Well yes, they got the message all the way back to Bien Hoa, the Special Force Headquarters. They weren't happy. Anyway, that was fun. What were they gonna do...fire us?

****

Sergeant Wergen and rat, Pvt. Dunning managed to buy some South Vietnamese army tiger-stripe uniforms before they were airlifted out to their Cambodian mission.

Wergen comments: The tiger stripes were what everyone wore on most special missions with the Mike Force. The U.S. Army hadn't issued any of those yet. So we had to get some wherever we could and then somehow make them fit.

Arriving at Camp Dunard, Wergen and Dunning linked up with a battalion (approximately 400) of Taiwan Chinese mercenaries from the "Mike Force" (Reactionary Mobile Strike Force) made up of several companies and battalions of various fighting groups located in at least three South Vietnamese locations—probably more, but mike force setup and location details weren't ever announced for obvious reasons.

The primary responsibility of the Mike Force was to support other CIDG and Special Force squads that might face sudden attacks while on a mission. They were also called in to bail out small teams of reconnaissance units who also might suddenly find themselves in trouble in some jungle location. The Mike Force would usually be the 'first in' to save and extract them from trouble. And they would occasionally fulfill other special missions such as this one.

Wergen comments: Over the course of my tour I was attached to the Mike

Force to carry out numerous special military operations; especially when we'd go from hot spot to hot spot such as the battles of Junction City and Manhattan to crush major enemy uprisings.

Operating under the umbrella of the Mike Force, these mercenaries—bearing the villainous skull and crossbones insignia on their fatigue jackets—were paid fifty cents a day while in camp, $50 for a captured AK-47, $75 for an enemy "kill" and $100 for bringing in a prisoner. They enjoyed earning their rewards and were much more eager to perform their job as hired guns, rather than guards or saviors. Wergen looked to them as assassins.

Wergen comments: These guys reminded me of another killing-machine unit we were once temporarily assigned to – the 101st Korean Tiger Division. One day we were taking a deuce and a half (2 ½-ton 6-wheel truck) to Tan Son Nhut airbase to bring back some recruits that were to replace their KIA's. I and a Korean Master Sgt. were selected for the commute because I could speak English and get us on base, and he could tell the Koreans what to do.

On the way back to base we drew some sniper fire and the Korean Sgt. asked me to stop the truck. He sent about a dozen unarmed men to find the shooter. About fifteen minutes later they came back with a carved-up body of the sniper. Oh…and they were quite proud that only two of them had gotten shot.

About a week later they caught a Viet Cong sapper planting explosive booby traps outside their compound. Well, over the front gate of their compound they had a couple of posts with an oriental looking cross piece to which they put the sapper, who they had basically skinned alive, on display. They watched as the mosquitos and other insects tortured and tormented that poor devil to a long and agonizing death. For sure, these foreign mercenaries of any origin were not ones to mess with.

This assignment at Dunard with the Mike Force mercenaries centered on a tactical portion of the notorious Ho Chi Minh Trail across the border into Cambodia favored by THE NVA and Viet Cong to move men and supplies into the area. The ultimate goal of the mission was to seed the destruction of the road once it was reached—plant land mines and leave.

Over the last few weeks, the rats and other supporting squads *had* been secretly working in Cambodia to map the area of the Ho Chi Minh Trail for attack. It was difficult as the gnarly jungle and lack of any decent charts or air visuals made pinpointing a critical position almost impossible.

Yet they were energized when they finally discovered a suspected stretch of critical enemy-traveled route—a simple two-lane road; although concealed under heavy jungle canopy, allowing the area and enemy convoys to escape common U.S. air surveillance and bombardment.

Sergeant Wergen in tiger-stripe uniform just before "Mike Force" Special mission

When they swiftly contacted base camp to report their crucial find to headquarters, they were instructed to promptly plot out the course and return to base to conduct land mine preparation. They would then return and destroy the road, of course to ideally cripple the movement of the enemy convoys.

While planning the mission strategy, U.S. headquarters decided that working with the MIKE Force would be more efficient by operating somewhat in their environment. The mercenaries would only have to learn the overall operation and strategic explosive handling with proper supervision, training and leadership. This is where Wergen's team came in.

Although teaming the *Rats* with the mercenaries usually proved quite valuable in serving the U.S. interests, there was frequently one major drawback—communication. The mercenaries spoke very little or any English at all and unfortunately the *Rats* weren't literate with their foreign tongue. It also proved awkward using interpreters on short commands or trite but critical instructions during training drills.

Consequently, with the wearisome war conditions putting tempers on edge and patience usually wearing thin, it was difficult enough for the *Rats* to communicate with each other, much more challenging to connect with foreigners. This problem was especially common with mercenaries whose main goal in life was to impatiently scamper around in the wilds on enemy death-hunts trying to become rich on abundant American dollars—not to hold conversations. But at end, the overall arrangement usually proved a winning combination for both units.

The mission at hand was going to be extremely demanding and dangerous not only because of the dense jungle potentially crawling with Charlie, but the American mission would entail hundreds of men penetrating Cambodia while heavily laden with ammunition and mines. And if any major trouble erupted, the men would basically have no maps, making their location almost impossible to determine; therefore, no Air Force backing to help get them out. Yet, there was no viable alternative—carry on with the operation and the war.

They soon moved the Cambodian mission preparation and training from Camp Dunard to Bu Dop, located in the far northwest corner of the Province, which was closer to the Cambodian border and closer into range of their prime target area. This would eliminate any need for a long-distance major air lift of that many troops by chopper, which would be more awkward and riskier yet. Instead, they would simply load up with ordinance and mostly march into Cambodia.

Then major apprehension set in at Bu Dop even before training began. Because of the U.S. communication limitations with the mercenaries, Wergen had requested his superiors show extreme caution and to provide graphic posters and *dummy* mines with *dud* fuses for their training, to avoid any serious exploding mishaps.

But to Wergen's dismay, he soon learned that no training aids were available and that live munitions would have to suffice. They'd all just have to be very careful while handling the explosives.

One of these mines was a *Bouncing Betty*, a type of in-ground landmine that detonates when pressure is been placed on it, mainly a footstep; of course careless handling could also set it off. After discharge, the mine springs into the air spinning and exploding, spewing shrapnel in all directions at head-level for maximum fatality effect. Any mistakes and this mine was capable of killing or seriously shredding everyone within a 15-meter radius. This unfortunate situation obviously left everyone uneasy, but they had to follow through with the plans. Again, carry on with the operation and the war. To add to the stress they were also using zero-delay hand grenades for the booby trapping operation.

Wergen comments: a normal warfare "pineapple" grenade has a 4- to 5-second delay built into the fuse; so after the pin is pulled and it's lobbed the safety spoon pops off and the delay is about that long before it explodes spreading death or serious mayhem through shrapnel. But the grenades we used for burying as booby traps had no delay…as soon as the safety spoon popped off…KFB! This no-delay situation obviously made us quite nervous when we were working with them for the mission…this is why we were so persistent about watching every individual to insure they did everything just so. We had carelessness and tension covered.

The strategy in planting the mine field in Cambodia was to have each mercenary carry five bouncing-betty mines to plant, and under one of them he would place a zero-delay grenade. And when he had the five-mine setup secured he would carefully pull the pin on the grenade and then cover up all his mines with dirt and leaves. Obviously this is a very risky and deadly operation to perform, especially when the planter has no idea of what is really going on *before* training.

For the next five days — using live mines and fuses — Wergen and his team showed the mercenaries how to place them, bury them and what the finished pattern should look like. Then the mercenaries would do it, place them and dig them up to start all over again. One mistake and many lives would be lost.

As feared, the communication limitations caused some harried moments and major stress during the training, but the mercenaries were trustworthy and combat efficient, so confidence remained high that things would work out well—trust *had* to remain high. And they were loyal and obedient, which enforced the heavily preached mantra of taking good care of each other. And that comradely interaction required little or no talking. Still, occasionally tempers flared and relaxation was basically non-existent. But they got through it.

Finally it was determined the mercenaries were ready and knew what to do so the mission was scheduled for the early morning hours two days hence.

Wergen comments: With the mercenary teams using live mines, and loaded zero-delay hand grenades to be used for booby trapping, it was an extremely strenuous period while training for our Cambodian operation. I believe that in all my life I never worked so cautiously at something while being absolutely scared as hell during that whole week, without any benefit of a common language between us and the mercenaries. Yes, we made it, but I was close to being a total basket case while working with that very serious ordnance...I caught very little sleep.

I remember the night before we left for Cambodia I asked a Special Forces medic for something to help me sleep...to unwind the taut spring of anxiety and adrenalin that had built up over the training period. He took one look at me, rolled up my sleeve and administered a shot without saying anything. I was leaning against the tent pole and the last thing I remembered was sliding down the pole as my world turned black.

I learned the next day they had given me Thorazine, because they were so worried about my anxiety and tension level. They said they gave me this powerful drug because that was the only thing available to help me and I was about to go on a mission where many lives were at stake. This was the battlefield. We had "carry on" covered.

****

On an early morning in January the Cambodian operation began for real. The mission mercenary battalion numbered approximately 300 men, led by a small team of American Special Force troops, including Wergen and Dunning.

Besides toting their weapons, everyone carried about twenty-five pounds of high explosives in their packs. As trained, the mercenaries responsible for the mine-setting were separated in to thirty-two 5-man teams, each carrying a minimum of five mines of different types and their detonating paraphernalia. The rest of the troops and mercenaries were used for security, supplies and leading the operation overall.

Laden heavily with the destructive weaponry, the battalion filled seven slicks and eight Chinooks to take them the short distance out of Bu Dop to the border LZ, where they began their march North into the Cambodian jungle to find and replace a stretch of critical Viet Cong supply route with a lethal minefield — compliments of the U.S. Special Forces. Luckily there wasn't much need for communication along the way with the mercenaries. They all just followed each other in line, sporting moderate smiles.

Wergen comments: Why the mercenaries were constantly smiling was a mystery to me, unless they were thinking about the American payday waiting for them back at Bu Dop. We met no major resistance on the way, which was a really good thing because any bullets in any of those bouncing bettys would be a really bad thing. Our lead scouts did find a couple of listening posts, but dispatched them with ease. We had mission progress covered.

On the second day they reached their objective — the heavily enemy-traveled trail section. With Wergen and Dunning moving fast and furious, they lead the way in mapping where the mine-clusters were to be placed.

Each mercenary team promptly went to work emplacing the mines and methodically setting the grenades to trip the mines when disturbed; a team also detailed-mapped the site of the minefields for possible future operations in the area, and for intelligence to follow the progress of this mission. The effort went smoothly, or so it seemed. With the mission objective finished, they swiftly returned to Bu Dop, again encountering no casualties or enemy resistance.

Not meeting any resistance surprised the U.S. team. But they had to credit *good luck* as the reason why — what else? When they returned to Bu Dop copies of the mapping were turned over to the ARVN and CIDG force for intelligence gathering and to keep observation on the mined road. They had mission completion covered.

Unfortunately, their elation over the success of the mission was short-lived. About a week later they learned from CIDG sources and the battle damage report (BDR) that after all they had gone through, a water buffalo had wandered into the minefield and tripped one of the mines blowing the poor animal to smithereens.

Wergen comments: We know it didn't take long for Charlie to figure out what was up. They surely must have carefully unearthed all our painstaking effort that had meant to deal them a major setback. They wouldn't have left that trail section to chance.

So I suppose this might be a lesson on how to risk your life while learning how to blow up a water buffalo using the extreme resources the U.S. military could muster for a single mission — including scores of Taiwan Chinese mercenaries and fifteen aircraft; and then supplying your enemy with hundreds of enemy mines.

****

This failed mission only added a more of a tense time for Sgt. Wergen — blowing up water buffaloes, facing tigers, though seemingly realizing no concrete progress for peace.

Yet the final stretch of his tour was about to become more horrendous for him, and actually the entire U.S. forces in Viet Nam. The predicted rumors of the TET Offensive was about to come true — and how so. They would have severe wartime covered.

Chapter Twelve

The Turning-Point Year—1968—Tet Offensive

The U.S. and South Vietnamese military were soundly snookered on January 30, 1968. Even though reliable intelligence had predicted that a major enemy assault might occur anytime from the end of 1967 on, they had little choice but to prepare for an expected thirty-six-hour cease fire that would signal a peaceful holiday truce to honor the TET Lunar New Year.

Although the American Command anticipated sporadic violations would erupt as usual during this annual ritual, a cease fire was ordered in all areas of allied occupancy except south of the demilitarized zone (DMZ) in Quang Tri Province. This exception was in response to a substantial communist buildup surrounding Khe Sanh air base—located in mountainous terrain less than ten miles from North Vietnam near the border of Laos—that had begun in the fall.

They were correct with that expectation. In late January 20,000 NVA troops attacked Khe Sanh where 5000 Marines and allied troops lay encircled. The isolated base and the hilltop outposts around it were under constant North Vietnamese ground, mortar, and rocket attacks.

Despite massive U.S. air power support the battle would rage on until early April when the fighting tapered to a stop with the base in ruins. Perhaps secretly bending under enemy pressure, the Marines would silently abandon the base. Both sides would declare victory yet the North laid claim to the base soon after and never relinquished control. When the siege began President Lyndon Johnson had ordered the base be held at all costs; another setback that was paving a turning point in the war—and wearing heavily on a weary Johnson.

****

By dawn on January 30 the TET offensive finally materialized in full scale as feared. All hell had broken loose in South Vietnam. An all-encompassing brutal enemy assault from all sides had suddenly begun in the northern and central provinces, and by nightfall in the Mekong Delta regions and the North's main sought after prize, Saigon.

A combined force of greater than 80,000 VC guerillas and the NVA attacked multiples of key provincial capitals, numerous cities, villages and hamlets. In addition, the enemy boldly raided a number of American military installations and the majority of airfields that supported the South.

In most areas the concentrated fighting would last for about three days; however, the assault on Saigon and Hue was at a bolder level. Both were under a more intense and unrelenting attack and the residual after effects wouldn't totally dissipate until March.

A siege of Saigon—the capital of South Vietnam—was the North's spearhead effort of the TET offensive. Not militarily strong enough for an immediate entire takeover, their goal was a chewing strategy of seizure—piece by piece. They were after Saigon's strategic military and governance arms such as the South Vietnamese army headquarters, the U.S. Embassy, Tan Son Nhut air base and Long Binh's main allied military headquarters.

The battering of Saigon began with a small force of Viet Cong sappers (covert commandos, especially trained in mines and demolition tactics) infiltrating the population to launch an assault against the U.S. Embassy and the Presidential Palace. One or two VC even made it inside the Embassy before they were rooted out and killed. The attacks of these key locations were quickly quelled, yet not without considerable American and South Vietnamese casualties.

Wergen comments: Just imagine how much more prepared and housed (hidden) the enemy would have been in the attack on Saigon if the mammoth eight-level tunnel, Akron, hadn't been discovered, gassed and flooded in October of 67. How about all those weapons we captured that would have been in the North's hands to use against us.

It's believed that the routing of Akron had a major effect on the outcome of the Saigon attack. Charlie may have been short approximately 5,000 well-equipped and armed men to carry out their quick assault which may have made the difference between a possible overthrow, instead of their ultimate failure.

The Saigon attack was in unison with battalions of Viet Cong amassing a brutal blitz at all corners and angles of South Vietnam. The U.S. powers had expected something major if an offensive would occur as predicted, yet nothing of this emboldened magnitude.

At Hue, eight enemy battalions (thousands of troops) infiltrated the city and fought the defending American force, which included three battalions of U.S. Marine Corps, three battalions of U.S. Army troops and eleven battalions of South Vietnamese (fortunately *more* thousands of troops). The 11th Cavalry — Black Horse Division — also played an integral role in the saving of Saigon and routing the northern troops.

Overall it would end up as weeks of bloody fighting before the American-led allies finally expelled the enemy who lost upward of 5,000 killed and captured, while American and South Vietnamese units lost over 500 killed and wounded.

Heavy fighting was also occurring in the region around the Special Forces camp at Dak To in the central highlands along with the continuing attack against the U.S. Marines Corps Khe Sanh, where the first stages of attack had materialized weeks before.

In all areas, the allies were being overrun. Finally, more U.S. Army troops under the new XXIV Corps headquarters arrived to reinforce the marines in the Northern Province and Khe Sanh with the enemy thinning for the time being.

****

Just before dawn on January 30, Sgt. Thomas Wergen and his rats had been jolted awake by the incessant chatter of gunfire from the AC-47 planes (dubbed *puff, the magic dragon*). Running out of their hooch, they saw off in the distance the gunships firing their three 7.62 mm guns at 100 rounds per second, 6,000 rounds per minute. With every fifth round being a glowing red tracer it appeared as multiple neon tubes lighting up the area between the plane and the ground. Wergen quickly realized this was from no ordinary battle. This was *the* major predicted onslaught—the anticipated *TET offensive* must now be for real.

Wergen had arrived back in Di-An on January 28. He had been on a TDY (temporary duty assignment) with a South Vietnamese engineering unit about twenty miles north of Saigon. Wergen was NCOIC (in charge of quarters for the night), so before he bunked to catch a few hours of sleep he had been busy running around the base perimeter making sure everyone on watch was alert.

At night during the TET Offensive, incessant chatter and sight of gunfire from the AC-47 gunships (dubbed *puff, the magic dragon*).

Di-An had been getting mortar and rocket attacks since Dec 2. And on December 23 there had been a light and futile ground assault against the base; therefore, they were somewhat ready for anything—they thought so, anyway.

Wergen comments: I remember my Tet beginning on January 30 with a major attack of approximately nineteen battalions of VC and NVA against Tan Son Nhut Air Base, while another major attack was being waged at a village about a mile away from Di-An, called Thu Duc, which had an ARVN base.

This coordinated attack was probably designed to cause distractions while they mined our roads and blew up nearby bridges to lock us up; Thu Duc was where the AC-47 gunships were shooting at dawn when we popped out of our hooch. The light show was an incredible sight. I only wish it had been staged on friendlier terms.

****

As the TET offensive raged on Wergen and his Rats were as busy as the rest of the U.S. military defending South Vietnam while trying to stay alive, whereas so many of their comrades were falling. They weren't sent to Hue or Saigon, but instead were desperately needed to help clear roads and the main supply routes through their base and surrounding strategic areas. They were working the non-headline war, sweeping the road for mines and ensuring the roads were safe.

That included many and *all* roads to Long Binh, Saigon and north where Route 1 (South Vietnam's main highway and main supply route) branched off to Route 13 (Thunder Road) on to Phouc Vinh reaching the southern tip of the Iron Triangle; then onward to Ben Cat, Lai Khe, Chon Tran, An Loc, and Quan Loi.

Di-An—located tactically between Saigon, Long Binh and Bien Hoa—was a complete and demanding military operation. It was the home of the 1st Infantry Division, the 101st Korean Tiger Division, the 168th Engineers, the 27th Land Clearing Task Force and the 11th Air Cavalry. Wergen and his Rats, also based there, didn't directly report to any of those commands, but they jointly helped manage construction and the overall security for all.

During the early days of the TET offensive Wergen and the rats were not only asked to support opening and keeping the roads secure in to and out of Di-An, but were also responsible for patrolling and securing their section of the base perimeter.

Wergen comments: Indeed, we were kept quite busy. All bases north of Di-An were continually dependent on truck convoys for their supplies. We regularly helped spearhead their protection while on route through Di-An and beyond. We would usually lead in a jeep that had a large white sheet on the hood, so our guys in the air knew to be cautious when they saw it.

The mission to move a convoy of supplies for the bases—usually a minimum of 500 trucks—would muster at Long Binh before traveling north through Di-An before lumbering on to Lai-khe, a relatively safe haven, where they would spend the night. Next was a nervous jaunt to Quon Loi, which was the most dangerous part of the trip because this area lay heavily in the hands of Charlie, and the route angle threaded through thick jungle foliage the entire way.

The North obviously knew Di-An was a critical byway to connect at least five large bases; therefore, during TET they arranged different offensive tactics. Rather than use manpower to mount a straight attack on Di-An and the surrounding bases their first strategy was to disrupt the main U.S. lifeblood supply lines. The Viet Cong had erected over a 100 mined road-blocks and in unison blew up key bridges. They particularly keyed in on blocking Route-1 just north from Long Binh.

The roadblocks and traps also kept the 1st Infantry Division bottled up without supplies or any means of mobility, except by foot. Therefore, initially Charlie had done an adequate job on Di-An and several other bases by keeping the troops tied down and strained. Subsequently every base within a twenty-five mile radius was attacked while the military was held thwarted, unable to get supplies to Di-An or any of the bases located north of them.

Wergen comments: This was a critical situation to say the least. It would be over a week until we had the roads and bridges open again for the movement of supplies.

Enemy supply bridge removed for good measure—extreme wartime measures.

The fighting at Tan Son Nhut air base went on for eight days until the troops were able to move about and branch outward. This relief allowed Wergen and his rats to spend the next four days sweeping for mines and clearing road blocks. When that task progressed satisfactorily they proceeded to inspecting bridges to aid the engineers in coordinating men and materials to repair them.

Their work was, of course, perilous; not only from the tedious concern of safely defusing the land mines and other deadly booby traps, but they were in the constant sight of enemy gunfire.

Wergen comments: It became quite un-nerving when gunfire is going on around you while you're trying to clear land mines or set charges to blow up and clear road blocks. So our gun-jeeps were kept quite busy attempting to suppress the shooting and shielding us and the load of explosives and detonators we were carrying.

We switched spots quite often, moving from the machine guns to the mines to the road blocks, taking pictures and noting the damaged locations on our maps to aid the synchronization with the engineers who would follow up with repairs and reconstruction. Long, busy and scary days but luckily we survived them again.

After the rats helped clear away the mines and road blocks they then spent the remaining time as foot soldiers joining the roving patrols trying to keep Charlie's head pinned down so the Engineers could get on with their work. They would also help defend any Special Forces camps in danger of being overrun so as to keep any useable weapons and materials out of enemy hands.

****

By late February the Communist leaders realized that none of their military objectives were being achieved — they were losing and began a calculated withdrawal. Although American and South Vietnamese losses were heavy, they had held on mightily with a determined defense and effective counter attacks against the North. By March the TET onslaught had dwindled to sporadic fighting around Saigon and its outlying areas.

The Tet Offensive proved a major defeat for the North. Their intentions to overthrow the South had not only failed on the battlefront, but they were also unsuccessful in bringing either an uprising or appreciable support among the South Vietnamese population.

Yet the TET offensive did inflict a stumbling block to the South's heralded *pacification program*, which was a grand strategy for the government to solidify as a self-sufficient body by eliminating communism and encouraging economic development and political restructuring. In fact, the aftermath increased the homeless refuges in the delta to approximately 160,000, adding an intense burden to the overall South's recovery effort by having to care for them.

****

Specialist 5, Harry Snelling of PSYOPS, of course, found no solace in the TET Offensive materializing as he and others of his department had predicted. He would end up running, ducking and grabbing his weapon just like every other American in Saigon when the North hit.

That morning he was groggy from staying up late the night before watching the parades and fireworks from a hotel roof. Crawling from his bunk he reached for his radio.

Harry Snelling comments: The first thing I'd do in the morning was to turn on my little transistor radio. I liked listening to Adrian Kronauer's Good Morning Vietnam show. But this morning, there was no radio reception as the battery was dead.

He shrugged off the radio silence, showered and dressed and lethargically began making his way to the PSYOPS compound in Saigon. He found it strange that the streets were completely empty, with an unusual eerie calm. He thought it odd as just about every morning the streets and alleys would be teeming with civilians — but not today. He crossed an alley and saw an armored personnel carrier with MP's on top manning machine guns.

Snelling comments: One of them shouted to me that there was VC all over the city and that other areas of the South were under attack...I started running for the compound.

As Snelling approached the compound he suddenly heard the sound of gunfire coming from the vicinity of the Presidential Palace. Seeing a few guys standing around with weapons, but not in an effective defensive formation, Snelling was confused as to the extent of the offensive.

Snelling comments: I didn't know what was really happening as I ran inside seeing there were about fifteen of our guys in the compound, but no officers. So one other specialist 5 and I were the ranking men there. We took charge.

They divided the men into two teams and decided to sit it out and they'd split in to watch shifts. Snelling took the first watch and positioned his team where they could support one another with interlocking fields of fire. Although major fighting was now breaking out in Saigon, nothing happened at the compound for the next 24 hours as they switched watch positions.

Snelling comments: At dawn the next day a sergeant rode up on his motorbike, smoking a cigar. The man did have a flair about him. Anyway, he told us he had heard that some VC forces were trying to escape the city by following the railroad tracks that ran behind our compound, and to be alert. Now I'm no Audie Murphy but it was just as nerve-racking sitting in that compound as being outside, so I decided to be proactive.

Unable to stay put, Snelling found himself leading a five man patrol outside and down the tracks. Moving slowly and carefully, suddenly the patrol heard two shots ring out — one right after the other. Snelling went down with his rifle flying one way, his helmet the other. With the other soldiers ducking down, one of them screamed he had been killed.

Snelling comments: The noise had barely registered when I felt something slam into my chest...or rather, the flak jacket I was wearing. The force knocked me down. When I heard the kid scream I was dead... I wanted to scream back, 'You dummy, I'm not dead!' But I couldn't make a sound from the minor shock and the wind was knocked out of me. Fortunately, they saw me moving and a couple of guys pulled me back in the weeds and grabbed my helmet and rifle.

In a few minutes I was breathing well enough to move with the patrol back up the tracks and into the compound. None of us ever saw who had fired the shots. When I got back to the compound, I started shaking so badly, that someone else had to take off my flak jacket. Someone dug a spent round out of it. The bullet had gone about halfway through. It left a bruise about the size of an egg on my chest. No Purple Heart thing, but it sure scared the hell out of me.

****

The Viet Nam war situation would never be the same for the U.S. even though they defeated the North in the TET Offensive — the enemy had gotten too close "to home." A new awareness of vulnerability was escalating as the bases were taking increased mortar fire. The Americans couldn't help wondering what would happen next time. Most realized the North wouldn't quit.

Wergen and the rats dig new bunker in Di-An to enter quickly from their hooch when shelling begins. It'll have electricity for fan and beer cooler.

Wergen and the rats decided it was time to tighten things up and proceeded to build a new bunker with multiple feet of overburden (rock and soil) to escape the increased shelling. The bunker would be quickly entered by sliding down a "fireman pole" placed in the corner of their hooch. Steps were built in the opposite corner of the bunker to step out when it was clear.

Wergen comments: We even strung electricity for a vent fan and a small fridge for beer. Although it was crude, the shelter proved damn good cover during the frequent shelling and mortar attacks.

I remember one incident in April when the bunker came in real handy. Di-An caught sixty-six mortar rounds injuring dozens of troops but there was no serious damage or fatalities in our sector. While sitting down there I knew I had to hang on while counting the days.

The rats remained in and around Di-An through February performing daily sweepings for roadway mines, along with laying some mines and booby traps of their own.

They reinforced the protective fences in the outlying areas and performed other mundane, but critical defensive work. Afterward they would rush back to base hopeful to find some water left in the showers before chowing down in the mess hall. They would spend the rest of the night in total darkness as they were in blackout conditions until further notice, or death, whichever might come first.

Meanwhile Hanoi was planning its next offensive. As the Americans expected, the North wouldn't quit fighting. They knew no other life.

Chapter Thirteen
The Turning-Point Year — 1968 — Into Spring

As the new year continued to unfold, 1968 would prove to be a decisive year for both America and Sergeant Thomas Wergen. There would be a major shift on how Washington would view and handle the war and Sgt. Wergen would begin to wind down his tour mainly with new and covert missions with the Special Forces. Both would be in store for surprises.

While still defending against the major communist TET offensive into spring, Wergen along with most everyone else in the military was stretched to their limit. He was moved from one firestorm to another with the MIKE Force, The 168th Engineers and any other unit where he could provide his assistance, which was usually where his demolition skills were needed.

Wergen comments: Even if I'd tried to keep a journal I don't think that I could have documented any details of the whole TET defense situation as we were all totally exhausted for a couple of weeks. We used to literally sleep for only minutes at a time, whenever and wherever we could; and that was usually only when we were moving from place to place by air, Jeep, or whatever means.

It's hard to believe that I could sleep soundly while riding on top of an APC in 100 plus degree weather, with the shelling noise and everything else going on. Who knows I may even have been shot at a few times. But catching that sleep was easily learned and really appreciated.

Gradually the TET offensive began winding down in America's favor — at least from a lessening blast-furnace effect. Wergen was still busily working his hectic assignments of clearing mined roads and general base guard patrolling wherever needed. But fortunately the duty was becoming manageable and somewhat straightforward.

Yet Valentine's Day of 1968 will forever remain horrendous for Sgt. Wergen. He had witnessed many tragic scenes during his war tour, but this one remains in his mind as probably the worst. That day mostly everyone but Wergen and Cowboy were out in the gunjeeps on patrol. Wergen was in their hooch mulling over maps for his next road assignment when Cowboy rushed in telling Wergen that he had received word that an enemy mine had been discovered on the motorway close to *the pit* by a couple of engineers, and they needed it defused — now.

Bien Hoa Base after TET

Wergen comments: The pit was a laterite — a rigid indigenous red clay used for road building — excavation center a few miles from Di-An, maintained and operated by the 168th Engineer Battalion. Incidentally the laterite clay was why the tunnels were so strong without shoring.

Wergen and Cowboy swiftly secured one of the few remaining jeeps, unfortunately without machine gun or radio, and swiftly drove toward the pit. There they met up with two rookie engineers who said they had spotted a mine in the road and would lead them to it.

Cowboy and Wergen began following behind their jeep toward the suspected booby trap when suddenly a KFB! erupted. Cowboy brought the jeep to a screeching halt as human body parts, metal fragments and flaking dirt suddenly rained down on them. Wergen quickly realized the engineers had hit a second mine they had luckily or unluckily missed earlier.

Although one engineer was barely alive when Wergen and Cowboy jumped from their jeep and began to administer first aid, they had no radio to call for a medevac support. Wergen and Cowboy worked anxiously to do what they could to stop the bleeding and maintain the young engineer's life, but to no avail. He soon joined his partner in death.

Wergen comments: That was a horrible scene. Not only was this kid dying in agony but we couldn't call for the emergency helicopter. I was blindly screaming into the air...I felt so frustrated and helpless. I never went anywhere without a radio again.

When the Engineer's also-young lieutenant heard the explosion he frantically rushed to the scene and started hysterically running up and down the road at seeing the scattered remains of his men. Worried that there were more mines in the vicinity that he might set off in his crazed rant, an equally manic Wergen struck him to the ground to stop him cold.

Fed up with war and fatigued, Wergen and Cowboy calmed and silently helped the medics to carefully sort out what parts belonged to whom, before quickly sliding them into body bags.

Sill silent in reflection, Cowboy cautiously drove them back to Di-An where they notified G&R (Graves and Registration) with the ghastly details of the kid's deaths and then proceeded to get drunk while they wrote letters home to their loved ones.

Wergen comments: I'll always hate Valentine's Day because of that incident...dammit!

****

In late February, General Westmorland would request 206,000 additional troops from President Johnson and his war cabinet. Perhaps to send a message to the world, however, a war-weary Washington would soon after approve only a quarter of the general's request—approximately 50,000 troops.

Regardless of Johnson's latest reduced troop approval, the overall U.S. military power in South Vietnam was mounting. It was estimated that by the summer of 1968 their troop strength would approach 500,000. The U.S. Army alone was growing to a peak of nearly 360,000. Up to now, more than a million American soldiers had rotated through Vietnam.

In addition, there were 61,000 other allied troops and 600,000 South Vietnamese armed fighters. Unfortunately, body-counts was the standard measure of success in the war; fortunately, America was winning on *that* measure with fewer points (counts).

****

In March Wergen was flown off by slick to a Special Forces camp in

Loch Ninh where he would begin and remain mainly assigned to the 5th Group 1st Special Forces on a variety of assignments until he rotated out for home. Some of the bases he would deploy from were Loch Ninh, Bu Dop, Dunard, Song Be, Prek Lok, Nui Ba Den and Tay Ninh.

Wergen comments: There were probably more. But I couldn't keep track of all the places they sent me. I had enough trouble staying awake during the journey. They probably could have sent me to Hanoi and I wouldn't have known…or probably have not even cared.

At first, he had no expectations of what would happen from wherever, or exactly whatever would be asked of him next. And that didn't really matter. He would do what he was told and serve out his remaining months. He wouldn't muddle himself with useless thoughts about *the why* of what he would be asked to do. Wergen only prepared himself for a lot more of war he knew he'd have to experience. He was right—a whole lot of war lay ahead.

He would soon find out that most of the missions of the Special Forces that he would participate in were to search out to engage enemy units and a secondary mission was to locate and liberate prisoners of war (POWs) of all allied forces, not only Americans. These missions were subject to careful reconnaissance and a strategic planning process for stages of the operation. Yet of all the success the Special Forces had in scouting and seeking out the enemy and destroying him, most the prisoner rescue missions were impotent, anything but successful.

Wergen comments: We mostly failed at rescuing POW's because of a combination of limitations. Faulty intelligence was often the case; taking too long to get there; security leaks beforehand; and, of course, simply not being able to find them. Keep in mind that we were mainly operating in thick jungle using only a simple compass and rudimentary maps.

Usually the squad could tell if they were just being set-up for an ambush because it was known the NVA didn't keep prisoners very long before they were taken west across the border, or up north to Hanoi. Most captured professional soldiers like Green Berets and Seals were just quickly tortured and killed, usually knelt down and executed with a shot to the back of the head. They were too big a risk to try to hold on to — not many of them ever made it to a POW camp.

Wergen comments: There was one other interesting thing going on. John McCain had been shot down in October, and there was always an anxious search for his whereabouts and we were always on an hour's call (standby) to try to rescue him if we found out. But we didn't, of course.

****

A tired and Jaded Wergen being air lifted to Special Force camp

One hectic March morning with the TET offensive still ongoing, word came from the 11th Cavalry unit near An Loc that one of their *Fire Artillery Support Bases* (a military camp to primarily provide major artillery support for infantry units out in the open) was under intense enemy ground attacks and it was highly anticipated that it was going to be overrun with a building enemy force.

The disappointed U.S. powers reluctantly conceded that they should quickly abandon the base, so that no personnel were lost and no equipment or weapons could be captured.

Wergen comments: This was a forward artillery support base located between a couple of 11th Cavalry units and was also close to a Special Forces camp. It was strategically positioned as to also support fire missions for other units in the area that needed help.

Unfortunately, the base was difficult to protect because it was actually about five miles from the units it was protecting. This is probably why the North was picking on it — low-hanging fruit.

Sergeant Wergen was asked to join a team which was put together to abandon and destroy the fire base, and while doing so set a trap for the onrushing but unsuspecting enemy when they sprang their ground attack. The plans were drawn up to be executed like a Saturday movie war matinee.

At dusk the destruction team quickly moved all valuable items from camp except for a few 81mm mortars and 105 mm howitzers that were set up to be easily seen by the North from the facing woods.

At the same time Wergen and his support team moved in to set charges designed to destroy the base, including the command bunker, mortar pits, tents, berms and everything else that could hold charges. Wergen and his men strung miles of detonating cord and several redundant fuses that amassed a charge of somewhere near 20,000 pounds of high explosives.

Meanwhile most of the base personnel were being slowly evacuated by Chinook helicopters at a landing zone far off into the foliage while a small guard force kept watch on an impending attack; another small force from the fire base stacked mortar and Howitzer ammo around the enemy (weak) side of the fire-base perimeter.

At dawn the jungle began coming alive with the first signs of an enemy attack. Wergen set the fuses before quickly slipping out of the compound with the remaining men. They rushed through the woods to the landing zone where they were picked up by the awaiting slicks and flown away. The base was totally unattended except for some stick rifles and helmets like guards on watch — and an exploding trap.

Wergen comments: As Charlie was near the camp a massive explosion incinerated a lot of them and of course obliterated the camp. We were airborne about five miles away and the pilot almost lost control of the slick from the shock wave of the blast.

We were lucky as most enemy assaults on base camps start with a barrage of mortar and rocket fire, and followed by a ground assault by masses of troops. But here they moved as close as they dared during the night and then attacked with little or no artillery, only masses of troops.

Anyway, we closed this base with a helluva bang. It was actually a spectacular sight from the air as we flew away.

Wergen laid his head back and caught some sleep as the slick raced toward An Luc and a day or so of non-warfare while he prepared for his next calling — a mission that would be a real surprise even when he thought he had seen and experienced it all.

Chapter Fourteen
1968 – Tet Counteroffensive Phase IV – May

In early May Viet Nam was being influenced by many factors. The monsoon season had arrived; the North attempted to carry out a second phase of their offensive against the South (dubbed the mini TET); and the initial peace talks were warming up in Paris. But the country was still all about war and blood.

Rainfall is infrequent and light in Vietnam except during the south monsoon season from May to September when rainfall is heavy. The torrential rain can limit sight to only a few meters for both day and night. Roads are washed out, trails become muddy quagmires, and most important, many times leaving only a skyline ceiling of 300 to 400 ft., eliminating any effective air support. Obviously, these influences have to be factored into any war strategy – whether defensive or offensive.

Wergen comments: I always felt the weather in Vietnam was made up of only two seasons, hot and wet. The wet season came along in May. But it didn't really help any.

Weather wasn't a factor on the Morning on May 5 when THE NVA and Viet Cong viciously attacked over 100 targets throughout South Vietnam, once again including Saigon. Yet by now the American and the South Vietnamese army were tolerating no more communist military surprises. They were much better prepared after experiencing the original TET Offensive and having paid more serious attention to the allied intelligence and the PSYOPS group.

So aided and warned by basic screening fundamentals, the allied forces were prepared and defended the cities with the utmost determination. Before the communist forces would reach their objectives, most of them were intercepted and decimated. Consequently Saigon was never in real danger of being overrun.

Yet thousands of enemy did manage to slither through the South's defensive line to once again plunge the capital into chaotic battles. Severe fighting occurred in the outskirts of Saigon – Phu

Lam, around the Y-Bridge, and at Tan Son Nhut. But the routing of the communist took only a few days and it was basically all over. The Northern forces withdrew from the area and fled to their sanctuaries leaving behind thousands of them dead.

On May 10 a world of hope (literally) emerged as the first peace talks—that would last sporadically for five years—between the U.S. and Hanoi began in Paris. But unfortunately those talks soon crumbled because the U.S. insisted that the northern troops withdraw from the South, and Hanoi insisted on Viet Cong participation in the coalition government in South Vietnam. These mandates were a non-starter for both sides.

****

Thomas Wergen felt proud and lucky during early May. He felt proud to have been promoted to Staff Sergeant in April and he felt lucky that he had now survived long enough in Viet Nam to enjoy a 7-day rest and relaxation period (R&R) that soldiers serving in Viet Nam were annually awarded. This short rest and relaxation period is not to be confused with the normal thirty-day leave a soldier annually earns. Even though he had that month of regular leave coming, taking it was strictly forbidden while serving in Viet Nam. Wergen selected Sydney, Australia from one of nine available destinations—none in Viet Nam.

It was amazing, however, that even in this war-torn country where friend or foe was indistinguishable there was one spot in Viet Nam an Army trooper could go and feel completely safe: a white sandy beach called Vung Tau located Southeast of Saigon on the South China Sea. Yet any R&R there was usually earned for special merit reasons—a rare "atta boy" reward that didn't count toward any earned annual R&R.

Wergen comments: I chose Sydney because I always heard it was fun there, and most everyone spoke English rather than choices like Tokyo, or Bangkok. And Hawaii was just too American. Hell, that place was for married men.

Besides being single and carefree on a week's vacation, I also wanted to experience a different culture. And I had a few dollars I could spend on an

Aussie lady…or ladies. And also I had an extra two days off for travel. But most important…I was out of harm's way to catch my breath and my wits. I guess that's what really mattered to me.

There was one good thing about the Special Force assignments that Wergen was serving on; he was readily back from the field after a mission, as most of them were short. So when his Australian slot became available he happened to be on base to receive his vacation orders.

Wergen comments: I could hardly believe it when I changed my piasters for dollars, and checked my weapons and fatigues in for dress Khakis to begin my travel to Australia. Only hours before I was fighting for my life.

He smiled when he was given his venereal disease check-up (an Australian prerequisite). *Yeah, sure*, he told them, a fat chance he would have contracted anything in this jungle warfare. But he understood and easily accepted Australia's requirement.

Wergen comments: I did have a Chinese/French girlfriend named Lin who I would visit occasionally at a bar not far from Di-An. She was sweet and spoke French, English and Vietnamese. And I ended up trusting her.

We rats used to drive to the joint for a break and back the gun jeep inside facing the closed door and there was always one machine gunner on watch, even though the place appeared closed from the outside. Anyway we'd anxiously enjoy some food, beer and whatever other "relaxation" we could muster up.

They had a steam room in the back where after a long tunnel-denial mission we'd hydrate with ample amounts of beer while we sweat out the laterite soil that was stuck in our pores. It was fun, but those times were too few and far between…but then, maybe that was a good thing.

That was as close to a situation for Saigon female companionship Wergen would even consider. A reckless soldier always provided a chance of being trapped into death—compliments of a North Vietnamese sympathizer. And during those days in Viet Nam, or actually any world combat duty anywhere, meeting American or "round-eyed" women was rare. Perhaps there might be nurses or well-guarded clerical workers occasionally in sight. But if they *were* available, they were usually socializing with officers as they were most likely officers themselves.

Wergen arrived in Sydney and was bussed to the R&R Center where he sat and anxiously listened to the welcome lecture before he was finally set off on his own. While there that week he thought about enrolling at the University of Sydney as a Chemist (pharmacist). He thought he could change his home address to Sydney and be sent there as his final duty station and then maybe even study to become a doctor.

Wergen comments: Yeah, I seriously considered the Australian doctor venture. But when it was all said and done I thought maybe I'd have seen enough blood after the Viet Nam tour. I was also getting homesick. So I decided I wanted to go back home to California when my tour was up.

He enjoyed his ideas of freedom during that week of enjoying drink and female merriment, and his escape from the hell he had been experiencing. But his real world of war soon loomed large along with the Viet Nam skyline as he flew back to return to Di-An. But then he felt he could do it some more, even though he had no choice anyway.

In fact, while in the air he thought more about volunteering for the three-month extension and be discharged from the Army for good in October when his tour would then be up. At first thoughts in Australia the idea of extending beyond June seemed crazy to him, but then only three more months…12 weeks…90 days instead of eight more months pulling some awkward stateside duty, with him having to put up with rank and a stringent military lifestyle he had little tolerance for anymore.

And would there *be a chance* he'd be sent back here anyway if he were still active back in the states? He wondered what this war holds for the U.S. and what deployment policies they may change over the coming year. And he knew if he extended there would be a lot of time spent on the administrative and paperwork procedures which would also shave off some time here.

By the time Wergen landed at Tan Son Nhut and was on his way to Di-An the extension option was making total sense. At least he rationalized so — he *would* apply for it.

Wergen comments: Perhaps I was dreaming but with the three month extension I thought maybe now as a Staff Sergeant I could farm out more missions to the guys and stay in Di-An in our newly dug bunker. I wasn't sure exactly what my promotion meant as it was all new...but...

Anyway, I felt it was better than having to try to get along in the civilian military for eight months...especially at some damn military base in Kansas...or wherever.

I knew staying was a further chance of getting killed, but every day was. I was getting used to it. We'd see if it would be a mistake. And besides the Paris peace talks were starting up. Who knew what calm that may bring, and how soon? Anyway, the decision was made – it was done.

****

Staff Sergeant Thomas Wergen had appreciated his R&R in Australia, but the fun quickly became a blurred memory as his first night back at Di-An he was made Sergeant of the Guard, which was immediate and tense duty. He was finding out a bit more about his promotion.

And only two days later he and cowboy were sent to Tay Ninh Provence to do join up with another Mike Force "hatchet squad." These squads were made up of various specialists throughout the area and assembled for special missions dubbed *sneaky petes*, which usually meant crossing the border for some covert operation.

Besides Wergen and Cowboy (the only rats) there were approximately thirty-six Special Force troops, and a few Cambodian mercenaries and CIDG (Civilian Irregular Defense Group) fighters. The mission objective was to locate a suspected small POW holding camp in Cambodia and liberate any and all troops while eliminating as many of the enemy as possible.

The mission turned out badly. No camp was found because either the original intelligence was faulty, or the enemy had been informed in advance of the raid. After returning to Tay Ninh, the thwarted team disbanded and the rats returned to Di-An – business as usual.

Wergen comments: These special MIKE force missions into Cambodia, Laos and North Vietnam were especially sensitive – undertakings that the

U.S. couldn't publically announce or politically support, and therefore kept very quiet. You know...like the old Mission Impossible TV series.

Again most were usually set up to recovering POWs or capturing enemy intelligence. But some hatchet squad missions were called to influence elections in the south by eliminating candidates not favored by the U.S. powers. These were usually not even discussed above a whisper.

A lot of the missions were rumored to be ordered verbally from General Westmorland, carefully trickled down the ranks with no backup documentation. Then one day we found out for ourselves who was giving some of those mission orders.

****

One day in late May at Di-An, Wergen and Cowboy received a request message from the 11th armored Cavalry brigade (black horse patched) commanded by Colonel George S. Patton III who were on maneuvers nearby. They needed the rats to deny a cluster of enemy tunnels that were giving them fits in the area where the brigade was camped.

The Rats were eager to help as the 11th Cavalry had just played a pivotal role in saving the major cities, including Saigon and Tan Son Nhut airport, during the TET offensive by fiercely crushing and routing the enemy out of their lairs and war sanctuaries. Soon after TET subsided the 11th Cavalry was awarded the *valorous unit citation* from the Secretary of the Army — an esteemed honor.

Wergen comments: This would be our second time working with the 11th Cavalry, but our first to work with Col. Patton. He was good to us and saw to it that we had uniforms, weapons and an adequate bunker to pitch our tent, which was greatly appreciated.

Our hidey-hole was actually a bomb crater and dug out laterally to provide adequate overburden to protect us from the rocket and mortar attacks.

The Rats had been there about a week and developed a good relationship with Colonel Patton while they destroyed some tunnels that had been quickly abandoned, and calmed.

Then one morning the rats were mustered to pack their gear and weapons to catch a waiting slick to meet up with a quickly assembled hatchet squad. They had no idea where they were headed as the pilot only received instructions after they were airborne. Wergen and Cowboy calculated they were heading near Tay Ninh Provence yet again and most likely another border mission. But they wondered why this one was so secretive, more than usual.

Wergen comments: Tay Ninh Provence and two mountains, Nui Ba Den and Nui Ba Ra are about sixty miles northwest of Di-an on Hwy 1, just about where Cambodia pokes into Viet Nam.

Incidentally, we had to get immunized every three months as that area was supposedly infested with the Bubonic plague. It's not enough we had to contend with Malaria and Dengue Fever.

The slick put down on a rough clearing atop a hill and the men quickly exited. They spotted and headed for a clearing where a large medical tent was set up and filled with stretchers, a generator and the rest of the squad of about forty men.

Wergen and Cowboy thought it strange they recognized no one on the squad, which again included some mercenaries. Wergen also quickly realized the rats weren't called in for any tunnel work. Why such a large squad to deny tunnels? But as always, Wergen asked nothing and said nothing, which was the mantra and mandate of most Special Force mission agendas he knew about, and had participated in.

Wergen notes: At least keeping my mouth shut was my mantra. As long as they supplied me with proper supplies and weapons, what the hell did I care what the mission was all about...I mean, what difference did it make how much I knew before we began?

A short while later a heavily armed chopper carrying General Westmoreland and his close aides, cautiously hovered before slowly touching down in the clearing. In utter surprise, the squad watched in awe as Westmorland disembarked, walked to an easel at the front of the tent, attached some charts and turned to face the squad to begin his briefing.

Wergen comments: We all had a feeling something was up with this mission from the start. But as soon as Westmorland arrived all the confusion was quickly cleared up. Again, it had been rumored he had personally directed some "sneaky petes." This proved it.

Westmorland went on to address the squad of men who sat anxious, rigid and stone silent. They knew this was obviously going to be an important mission, and ultra-death defying. But then, what mission of this type wasn't?

He began explaining how the members were selected purposely with each being a stranger for complete secrecy reasons, and each had special skills and knowledge — the mercenaries were added for their knowing the country and their bloodthirsty attitude.

The general further explained that a CIDG team had spotted what appeared to be a bustling NVA R&R camp about six kilometers across the border, into Cambodia. Our mission was to cross the fence, find and strike-destroy what we could of the physical camp and kill as many of the enemy, before rushing back to the border where a substantial Mike Force unit would be waiting to ambush the large throng of pursuing enemy.

Wergen comments: What this amounted to is we were to be used as mainly bait to get Charlie as close to the Viet Nam border as possible, before they were to be ambushed.

Cowboy raised his hand and asked how many of the enemy did they estimate were in the camp. The general answered a reinforced battalion of about 6,000 men.

Expecting and seeing the bewildered look on the faces of the squad, Westmorland quickly added that it would be nice to have an Army (25,000 men) accompany them, but that wasn't practical, or politically wise. And even if so, Charlie would then just evacuate the area anyway.

Westmorland repeated the key strategy was to execute a "hit and run" maneuver by the squad and then the trap is sprung at the border, hopefully to crush the oncoming NVA. They weren't to be heroes. Just shoot and run like hell.

The general finished by having the squad mark their maps with the estimated location of the NVA camp and that a Chinook would be arriving soon with food, weapons and supplies. And finally, he told them to eat, get some sleep and be ready at 5:30 a.m. when the slicks would be there to pick them up to drop them as close as practical to the border.

He wished them good luck, turned and hurried to his waiting chopper and departed, while all the squad members sat looking at each other as the experience and mission strategy all sunk in.

At dusk a Chinook arrived and each fighter of the squad loaded up with two 66 mm. M72 LAW *(light anti-armor weapon)* rockets, two M2 20-lb. assault demolition satchel charges, 1,000 rounds of ammo, 2 quarts of water and some rice candy.

The assault plan was to surround the enemy camp in a half moon, each fire their M72 rockets and then empty two M-16 magazines before retreating. As they raced away Wergen would then drop and detonate his satchel charge with each man dropping theirs (numbered) at one minute intervals to slow down the chasing enemy.

Wergen comments: You'd think that with all the planning, bluster and bravado, the Cambodian operation would have succeeded like a Saturday matinee war epic with the good guys. It didn't. The mission ended up a real mess...things quickly turned to dirt.

At dawn the slicks arrived to pick the squad up and dropped them off on a ridgeline which was supposedly located six to eight kilometers from the combat objective. The squad would find out not so — by a long shot.

Unfortunately the terrain was not what was expected, or as straightforward as originally thought. The topography was uphill and then downhill and through the river; perhaps six to eight kilometers on the map in a straight line. But this tortuous march was *hardly six* to eight kilometers while hiking and negotiating the trails.

The trudge ended up more like an estimated twelve to fourteen kilometers when it was completed. And with each man carrying the weight of rockets, ammo, satchel charges, water and rice the whole trek was a constant struggle for all.

Consequently the squad did not make it on schedule. It was too late in the day and everyone was too exhausted to effectively carry out any attack plan. They would have to rest overnight and reform the attack at dawn.

But their communication with point command had to be scant in enemy territory and became confused. What the squad didn't know was the MIKE Force—who was to support their retreat—thought the mission had been abandoned and had scrapped their part of the strategy. They wouldn't be at the border.

Unknowingly, the squad would be alone and left to attack the camp and then try to outgun and outrun a reinforced battalion of really nasty NVA without any waiting support.

Wergen comments: We had no idea we had been left alone. We were all so sweaty, hungry and exhausted to really think about it I guess. We just unloaded our gear and found a place in that damn dark jungle to try to sleep.

Of course, if we had known what we would be facing the next day we would have turned around and gone back – pronto.

The next morning the squad crept in close range of the enemy camp and formed their half-moon killing blitz. And when given the signal, everyone fired their two LAW rockets and then each sprayed the perimeter with two magazines of ammo, turned and sprinted for the border.

But Charlie was alert and like a swarm of angry bees protecting their hive, they began a frenzied pursuit. The squad wasn't expecting their fierce counterattack—at least not so quickly.

As the squad bounded through the jungle Wergen was the first to drop his satchel charge, and each man of the squad knew their number, therefore in order, would follow suit at one-minute intervals until all had been dropped. The charges slowed Charlie down but didn't stop them.

The retreating squad radioman finally made contact with their C&C (command and control) ship, frantically shouting a request for them to contact Tay Ninh artillery to lay down a barrage to assist the squad in gaining some clearance between them and a surging Charlie. And to notify the Mike force at the border they were coming—unknowing that they weren't there!

The C&C contact soon answered that the Tay Ninh base battery commander refused to fire across the border into Cambodia. The situation was becoming deadly desperate for the squad as their ammo was running out.

Fortunately Colonel Patton, who had heard the transmission while airborne in his slick, ordered the battery commander to fire. When the commander hemmed and stammered, a furious Col. Patton promptly relieved him of duty, demanding the battery executive officer to fire, who immediately yielded to the colonel. The huge 175 MM self-propelled Howitzers were immediately readied and turned in the direction to support the squad.

The squad then received more anxious news. The battery could only fire one *spotter* round before receiving corrections from the squad before they could effectively fire a killing volley. Thus when the *spotter shell* was fired the Tay Ninh batteryman would yell "shot" and the squad radioman would yell "splash" when the shell hit, noting the time of flight and then proceed to give corrective coordinates near the target.

A 175 howitzer team (U.S. War Photo)

Meanwhile the squad had entrenched themselves in the woods and returned fire and grenades to slow down the enemy.

The squad's relief was again dashed when they were told after the *spotter* shot finally "splashed" it would be 92 seconds from the time it was "shot." So could the squad themselves survive an *effective* enemy-stopping artillery barrage? This shell has a kill radius of approximately 200 meters so the distance between the squad and Charlie was critical once the coordinates were set. Simply, the overall coordination of the artillery fire hits and the squad's escape zone had to be carefully calculated in this chaotic war setting.

Wergen comments: This was bad. First we were really outnumbered and fighting to live while waiting for the artillery support that we knew was the only safe way out of there. And that had to be timed just right or we could all be blown to hell.

Everyone ducked down by a tree as we finally heard the roar that sounded like an onrushing train, come over the tree tops and exploded like a fireball when it hit. I'm sure that woke Charlie up and slowed them down some.

It was calculated the spotter shell hit about 300 meters behind the squad. So the radioman quickly coordinated a drop of 200 meters (closer, into the enemy kill zone) and to fire a nine-round killing volley. He then yelled to the crouching but alert squad that after he yells "shot" give it 45 seconds then everyone run toward the border — and nine will be coming.

Wergen comments: We heard the radioman yell "shot" so we all threw all of the grenades we had, including smokes, and fired a few rifle bursts until the 45 second mark. We then ran like our lives depended on it...literally. We hit the ground seconds before what sounded like all hell had broken loose. After the 9th round we lit out again for the border.

Tay Ninh artillery also fired smaller consistent H&I (harassment and interdiction) artillery to keep Charlie on their toes while the squad just kept on running for the border. They had no choice.

When the squad finally reached Tay Ninh there was now an American blocking force of sorts that had been thrown together that was strong enough to scatter the NVA's further advance.

Wergen notes: Of course we were pissed when we found out the original Mike force had left the day before. But we also knew it was miscommunication. Anyway, we made it back, compliments of Colonel Patton. I wanted to thank him but he'd already left the area.

They ended up losing three of the squad. They estimated the enemy lost hundreds, as usual. But as always, they had just kept coming and coming. After the squad was debriefed Wergen and Cowboy returned to Di-An just in time to shelter down against a major mortar attack. It would be another sleepless night, until finally at dawn they were able to catch some much needed rest.

Wergen comments: That was the only mission occurrence I ever had with directly seeing General Westmorland. But I'm sure there were plenty of missions I was on where he had been in direct contact with the squad leaders.

Anyway, on July 1 he was replaced as U.S. commander in Vietnam by General Creighton Abrams. And if Abrams was ever associated with special missions I never heard about it.

Chapter Fifteen
Di-An — Tet Counteroffensive Phase IV — June

The climate was wet and the atmosphere strained in South Viet Nam as the TET Offensive battles were slowly winding down as America along with the allied troops were now strongly entrenched in an aggressive posture. During May and early June they conducted a number of major operations to crush the communist aggression.

In May they had totally liberated the Khe Sanh Combat Base enabling the South's allied forces to open Highway 9 for the first time since August 1967. This operation not only significantly constrained the North's use of western Quang Tri Province, but had caused mass casualties on two NVA divisions as they withdrew from the area.

The North was clearly on the run, yet they weren't quitting. They launched a ferocious attack on the Bien Hoa military holding compound, which was mainly used as a central facility within the country for the never-ending transfer of militia coming and going. The complex was constructed of buildings with tin roofs, concrete floors and wood-slatted partitions fitted with outsized screens to let in whatever breeze might be available to blunt the stifling heat — hardly well-fortified structures.

When the compound was barraged by enemy artillery, a few of the buildings had taken direct hits from the devastating rockets. A number of military men who were either rotating *out* of Viet Nam for home or entering the country for the first time were killed or badly wounded. It was a hellish time for both once-happy "short-timers" leaving, and the nervous "newbies" coming in.

****

A weary and tense Staff Sergeant Wergen sat in his hooch looking out at the damp overcast thinking about the Bien Hoa attack while again vacillating over a three-month tour extension to allow him to close out his military obligation for good. *Right*, he thought. You spend your tour here fighting for your life, constantly in harm's way; then when you believe you're bullet proof you go to Bien Hoa to catch your ride outta here, and you buy the farm there.

He wondered what his outcome could be no matter what he decided; killed today on patrol; killed in Bien Hoa waiting to leave, or killed at home in California crossing a busy street. Extending had been an easy decision while he sat in that friendly Australian bar with no bullets flying around his head—do it...extend. He had made his decision.

But now after that Special Force "sneaky pete" in Cambodia last month where the big-gun howitzers had to bail out the squad during their escape back to the border, he wondered how much longer his luck would hold out.

And everything in the United States was a mess with Robert F. Kennedy just being shot dead in California after winning the primary for the upcoming presidential election. How would that incident affect America, and the upcoming months of fighting, if at all, as Kennedy was definitely against the Viet Nam war? Now Kennedy and that major war influence were gone.

Wergen comments: Yeah, I kept going back and forth after first deciding to extend while on my Australian R&R. Obviously being young and impatient I had to weigh this out carefully. If I rotated out in July I'd have to do some stateside military base for eight months.

But if I stay here three more months the chances were that much greater I end up dead. But since I was single and only responsible for myself a lot of the edge was off. And then I found out where I'd go for sure in the states to finish my duty if I didn't extend. After that the decision was easy...or easier, anyway.

Thomas Wergen was officially told where he would be sent to complete his active duty in the United States if he didn't extend in Viet Nam—an aging naval air station in Olathe, Kansas. The Pentagon was planning to close it down, which would require substantial engineering and ordnance labor, besides extensive chemical studies for different types of pollution such as lead and asbestos. And the base had been in operation for about fifty years so the possibility of toxic hazardous materials was an acute likelihood.

Wergen was mindful of the growing awareness of asbestos poisoning. Yet regardless of that risk, Wergen had no interest in spending eight months in a humid-continental climate—frigid winters and hot summers. He'd had enough of inclement weather. And he simply didn't relish the idea of any further stateside military duty of saluting, eating in mess halls and the like. Therefore, he finally officially extended his Viet Nam tour.

****

House at Four-Corners hiding Viet Cong planting above ground Claymore mines — about to go down (below)

South Vietnam and Staff Sergeant Wergen were in repair mode during June and July cleaning up from the TET offensives. Wergen and his rats were assigned damage reconnaissance duty with the 168th Engineering group, besides completing his extension administrative paperwork procedures. It was a welcome and fitting start for him now that he'd be here until October.

Wergen and the rats had use of a small bubble chopper to inspect roads and bridges to help determine the destruction levels. If the damage to roadways or structures was severe, they helped design alternate travel routes, including mine-sweeping duties. It became a daily routine.

With the fighting in the South subsiding in July, a new allied troop endeavor called *The Phoenix* program was established and begun to crush secret Viet Cong infrastructure (VCI) in South Vietnam. This new defensive effort would be no small undertaking, as the infrastructure had an estimated strength of up to 70,000 Communist guerrillas, who were responsible for a long-standing campaign of terror against Americans, South Vietnamese government officials, village leaders and innocent civilians. One day

Wergen and his rats got a chance to participate.

Wergen comments: Yes, we got our chance one day to participate in Phoenix, I suppose. There was a town-hall type of building at a busy intersection called four corners on the road from Di-An to Long Binh.

Charlie was forever placing large above-ground claymore mines here and we all got real damn tired of it. So one day we took a D-9 dozer there and wound the winch cable around the building and drove away, which cut through it like string through a cake and brought it crashing down. No more mines were planted in that area.

Although any and all duty in South Vietnam was precarious and dangerous for Americans, even road reconnaissance work, at least Wergen felt lucky that he was spared the Special Force border missions—for the time being, anyway. He knew better about it lasting.

Chapter Sixteen
Di-An — Tet Counteroffensive Phase IV — August

In August 1968 South Vietnam was hot, humid and much wetter creating a sticky and muddy environment from the usual jungle dust beds. In the United States the summer atmosphere was also hot, both literally and figuratively. Turmoil and bitter unrest was the rule with thousands on college campuses, city streets and at all political venues, protesting the war.

The reports were that the U.S. government's "freedom from communism" benefit of war was growing thin and had worn brittle with much of America. Their animated cry implied they saw little or no value in losing more men and women for a foreign cause that most really didn't understand, or really appreciate; and most just wanted it over and done with.

Richard Nixon — just nominated as the republican presidential nominee — agreed in principle and promised to bring an honorable end to the war in Southeast Asia if he were elected

Yet despite the American dissension at home, Staff Sergeant Thomas Wergen was in a recharged mode. He was preoccupied with beginning to see the light at the end of *his* tunnel, so to speak; and the bright lights of his California home shown brighter in his mind.

Now into serving his extension period, he was already being labeled as a short-timer by some. Moreover his recent duty of damage recon assistance work had been mundane, compared to the earlier Cambodian "sneaky pete" perilous duty he had participated in.

He had just completed seven days of recon labor on 85 kilometers of road and assisted writing a comprehensive report to send to the engineers for needed repairs. The effort was necessary in order to move a large 11th Armored Cavalry convoy northward. Making life easier for the 11th was another reason he enjoyed it. He hoped that for the rest of his time here this is the type of duty he would do. But he knew he was probably kidding himself about that—he was.

To add to his refreshed outlook he was happy about getting a chance to meet up with his lifelong friend that dated back to California grade school, Sergeant Michael Blackman, a combat MP (military police) based in Tan An with the 9th Infantry Division.

Wergen comments: Things were looking pretty rosy…well, as rosy as can be expected at that time in my tour, anyway. I only had a few months left to serve…no special force assignments on the horizon and I had arranged with my superior S-2 officer for a couple days off to go to Tan An for "special recon" work.

According to him, all I had to worry about was getting there and back. Of course, now that I thoroughly knew my way around the system that condition was easy to arrange.

When Wergen knew the timing was right, he organized his plans to hitch a ride on a C123 out of Tan So Nhut to Dong Tam where Sergeant Blackman would pick him up and they would go to *Tan An* for a couple days of "special duty." But as always in this country, sudden changes were the rule. And they weren't in charge of surprises.

Wergen didn't know then his quick trip would end up as a harrowing ARVN incident on the way to Tan An. And then his stay would end up on patrol with Blackman, not a bar-hopping outing. And that his plane trip back to Di-An would be another traumatic war experience.

Sergeant Blackman comments: I happened to be at Dong Tam when Wergen called me. We were having trouble with the connection and could hardly complete a sentence before a signal corps guy would keep coming on the line asking, "Working…Working?" It was funny, but frustrating as we couldn't really complete a thought. Perhaps that was a sign of things to come for his visit.

Tom asked me how the roads were…meaning were they open and safe. That was a strange question to me because in the 9th Division the state of the roads made little difference to us MPs. We ran them all the time…regardless. I said they were fine when in truth I had no idea. But I didn't want any reason for my good friend to maybe postpone his plans.

And Staff Sgt. Wergen realized after the call that the question about the roads was pointless. As there were no front lines in Viet Nam, he knew *anywhere* was always dangerous. And he would have to find out first-hand about the Tan An roads when he was there; and if their "special project" would turn out to be such a fun jaunt as they were planning.

Wergen comments: Yeah, I guess it was kind of a dumb question. Nowhere was ever totally safe. I always had my .45 and a small .22 back-up wherever I went. Hell...I even took my .45 to the shower in Di-An, my home base. So I could only hope that this visit would turn out to be somewhat relaxing as I completed my plans for the flight out of Tan So Nhut.

****

An excited Staff Sgt. Wergen landed at Dong Tam where his close friend, Sgt. Blackman, was there as planned to take them back to Tan An for a couple days of fun—their special project.

After a few hearty hugs and handshakes, Wergen jumped into the jeep and they headed to Tan An chatting and joking about anything and everything, while they both agreed that since there was traffic on the roads they were at least "open." But as they also agreed, "safe" was another matter. But they knew their traffic assumptions meant little as they were still in the military in a hostile country fighting a war. That's the only thing that was *for sure*.

Wergen comments: Oh yeah it was a great moment to meet up with my close friend from home. We were looking forward to a couple of days of drinking and carousing. But as usual in wartime, things don't always go as planned – what's new?

Suddenly Blackman jerked on the wheel, sharply pulling the jeep over to the side of the road. Wergen instinctively pulled his .45 and followed Blackman's gaze toward some smoke rising from behind the thick road foliage and heard some faint frenzied voices. They needed to investigate as perhaps it was an American or allied soldier in trouble, and hopefully not an ambush. And as an MP, this was Sergeant Blackman's responsibility as he patrolled these roads on a regular basis.

They slowly drove further into the brush until a crashed ARVN war vehicle came into view, wedged on a fallen tree branch. Blackman stopped the jeep and grabbed his M-16 from the back seat. With Wergen toting his .45 they jumped from the jeep and followed the noises as they cautiously hurried into the vegetation.

They stopped at seeing two South Vietnamese soldiers writhing on the ground badly wounded, helpless but appearing conscious. Two Vietnamese in civilian garb were pulling items from the soldiers' pockets while another was tugging at a ring trying to get it off one of the soldier's finger.

Although Blackman and Wergen had no idea at what or who was responsible for the assault, the Vietnamese bandits didn't appear armed so Blackman raised and pointed his weapon at them in a ready stance while Wergen shouted and fired his pistol into the air. The Vietnamese stopped, looked up and then took off running. *Sgt. Blackman comments: Those Vietnamese guys scattered like roaches in the beam of a flashlight.*

I was disappointed we had to stop and go through this when Tom and I were having a good time...especially when all he had was that .45 and a pea-shooter backup .22...and more scary when we had no idea what we'd be facing when we headed into the bushes. But I knew he didn't mind, sometimes we were also humanitarian agents in this terrible war zone.

Wergen and Blackman quickly headed back for the road and their jeep, while keeping an eye out for any armed Charlie that may be lurking, although the conditions with passing traffic watered down that concern.

Wergen grabbed the radio and yelled to Blackman that he'd call Dustoff (specific call sign for medical evacuation slicks) and asked if there were any colored smoke grenades in the jeep. Blackman answered negative. Wergen was on the radio while Blackman waved down a passing American army truck, asking for a smoke grenade. The truck driver had two — but they were both colored red. Not good, but they had no other choice if they were to make the medical transfer go at all. He ran over and handed it to Wergen with a grimace, then turned and readied his weapon to concentrate on guarding the perimeter.

Wergen comments: Red was bad. We used different colored smoke grenades to signal and pinpoint zones for air strikes, artillery and medical evacuations. The problem was that red was pretty much reserved for free-fire-zone which was commonly related to a hot extraction... or simply, "enemy target-shoot here." This made pilots nervous when reds were used for other purposes. So in this case I would have to carefully explain... and quickly.

Yet just identifying *any* color for *any* reason might not be enough when Dustoff showed up. A lurking Charlie sometimes employed a shrewd maneuver. He would listen to the Dustoff push (radio frequency) and when an American would toss smoke to isolate the desired position, Charlie would also toss one, hoping to confuse or induce a helicopter pilot into a deadly ambush. Therefore, the pilot had to determine *who* threw what, and where.

Blackman comments: The large medical red-cross emblem on an unarmed chopper meant little or nothing to Charlie at this point in the war. The standard procedure was that the pilot identified the color he saw thrown and then you had to immediately confirm that was the color smoke you threw. If they didn't match, things got pretty wild until they were sorted out...usually in the middle of a fire fight.

And regardless of the situation it was always dangerous to be around red smoke – period. I was really concerned the pilot may not even stop...but I left all that up to Wergen.

Wergen spotted the approaching medical slick and tossed the red smoke grenade.

The pilot barked: "Identify red!"

Wergen immediately confirmed: "Red thrown! Red Thrown...wounded ARVN!"

The pilot replied reluctantly he wasn't staying long and cautiously began his descent. Wergen ran to one of the injured soldiers, and Blackman to the other. They lifted them while the Dustoff slick bobbed like a yo-yo a few feet off the ground. In the brief moments of action Wergen and Blackman slid the wounded ARVN soldiers into the helicopter's cabin and quickly backed away as the slick swiftly ascended, making a steep-turn exit into the cloudy sky.

Wergen and Blackman swatted some blood and mud from their fatigues, grabbed their weapons and ran to the jeep to make their speedy intense exit, just as the slick had done.

Wergen Meets up with lifelong friend. Sergeant Michael Blackman, combat MP serving in Tan An

On the road back to Tan An base Wergen asked Blackman what the platoon emergency frequency was in case he needed to contact the base. He shrugged, looking sheepishly at a surprised Wergen.

Blackman comments: I knew Tom could not believe we would be running around without knowing our push, but he was kind about it. When we got to Tan An, I quickly stepped into the Provost Marshall's office and learned the frequency.

Wergen counter comments: Well, I just felt it was just one of those little misses that could get you killed. The radios we had back then were not that powerful and not knowing the nearest frequency could put you in serious jeopardy...real quick.

Also on the way back they decided they had had enough excitement for one day and decided to simply share a few beers on base that night, and forget any "grand tour" of downtown Tan An. And then the next day they would simply lounge around the base before Wergen was to head back to Di-An. They decided they needed no more surprises. But then they found out they still weren't in charge of surprises.

****

Early the next day Wergen and Sgt. Blackman were relaxing in the mess hall after morning chow and Blackman's superior approached the table and informed them that the wounded ARVN soldiers reported that there was armed Charlie in the area where they were shot—and that the threat would probably grow. So Sgt. Blackman was told he had to patrol the adjacent village on a search and destroy mission—today.

As his superior left, Blackman shook his head in disgust and looked over at Wergen who shrugged and stood, deciding to join the patrol providing he could find an adequate weapon.

Reaching Blackman's hooch, Wergen waited outside as he went in and soon emerged carrying a single pump 12-gauge shotgun, his fatigue pockets overloaded with shells.

"It cuts through the bush real easy," he remarked with a smile. He then handed Wergen his M16 as they headed for the jeep to return to the area they had found the ARVN soldiers. They spent the afternoon chatting and searching, but found no Charlie. They weren't disappointed.

Wergen comments: So this was my "relaxing" visit with my close friend, Sergeant Michael Blackman. We run into a potential battle on the first day and the next day we top it off with a search and destroy mission traipsing through mud. Oh well, it was still great to see him.

****

Adding to Wergen's drama, the plane from Dong Tam to take him back to Di-An was shot up while taking off. Fortunately, the damage was minor enough so that the pilot was able to limp the plane back to Tan so Nhut where they experienced a slight crash landing. With the base fire brigade standing by with emergency equipment to put out any fire, everyone scrambled out. A weary Wergen then hitched a truck ride back to Di-An.

Wergen comments: I escaped another incident. I was now beginning to mark the remaining days off my calendar. I wondered how long my good luck would hold out. Maybe I'd do just recon work from here on out… just maybe…I hoped.

Chapter Seventeen
Di-An—Tet Counteroffensive Phase IV—September

In September 1968 there was no warfare pause in Viet Nam or in the United States. In both countries the bloodstained battles were vigorous, varied and plentiful. Hanoi's forces were holding strong in the South and the 900th U.S. aircraft would be shot down over the North. And in America the drumbeat around the war protests continued to grow.

The remnants remained from the anti-war frustrations that had risen to battles between protesters and police at the democratic national convention held in late August. Chicago was the bloody U.S. frontline where over 10,000 angry protesters had gathered on downtown streets demanding the war be ended. They were challenged by 26,000 equally angry police and national guardsmen—along with hordes of civilian war supporters. The brutal confrontation was covered live on prime time television when over eight hundred demonstrators were injured and arrested.

The United States was experiencing a level of major nationwide turbulence. During 1968 there had been hundreds of student protests at colleges and universities throughout the land. The country hadn't been this divided since the civil war. And no end to the unrest was in sight as the horrific images of bloody mayhem and American military deaths were broadcast nightly on television into living rooms across America and the world—in vivid color.

Toward the end of September, Staff Sergeant Thomas Wergen was experiencing a myriad of emotions as he reached over and scratched out another day on the small calendar taped to his footlocker. He felt lucky he hadn't been in one of those nightly harrowing broadcasts in America—so far, anyway. He was excited and looking forward to honorably ending his Viet Nam tour in early October. He felt no guilt over that, as he believed he *had* and *was still* paying his patriotic dues. He felt he had achieved as much triumph and honor against the enemy odds as anyone else here.

Yet, as usual, he was antsy and anxious over knowing that until separation in Bien Hoa every minute here still posed a chance of finality. He wouldn't become complacent. Little things were important under his control. All he wanted to do was safely play out each day of the next few weeks by ear and leave in October without the detriment of a government issued metal coffin. He would not regard that an easy feat. He was still in demand. But he didn't want to take any more chances, especially after the sneaky pete and fierce gun battle he had found himself in last week, and almost bought the farm again. And he had thought he might be done with these special missions after extending his tour especially with only a few more weeks to go. He recalled the episode over and over.

****

Sergeant Wergen was disappointed he had to leave his road recon work and join another pursuit and destroy mission just inside Cambodia. He was to join the 5th Special Forces group because they thought the search may include tunnels.

The scene was tense as the further the squad got into their mission the more they knew the area was full of Charlie and any captured war prize was not worth the gamble. After losing one KIA to a Punji man-trap the squad chose a wiser move — get out.

They had given up the mission and were heading back toward the border and the landing zone for pickup. Marching slowly through the jungle using the toe to toe maneuver, they were being extremely careful because there was a lot of dry brush and bamboo that had been protected from the rains by the heavy tree canopy — a very noisy environment.

Wergen comments: Again, walking toe to toe means stepping on your toes and the balls of your feet, not putting down your sole or heel. This really makes you alert and sensitive to your surroundings. Of course it was tough after a few miles, but if it means your life, you endure it.

As feared they were suddenly ambushed by a large NVA raiding party. Normally under Ho's rules of warfare they would not have fired first but the squad's travel route had backed them into a corner and they had no choice but to battle it out. Or at least Charlie used that as an excuse to pick the fight. Their attack came from downhill.

The squad immediately planted themselves on a mesa where the ground went up steeply before the edge dropped off. This meant that when the NVA got to the top, instead of seeing a field they saw sky and had to look down to see us.

Wergen comments: They charged uphill to surprise us. My position was to guard the right flank and when the shooting started I wedged myself against a little tree and threw my pack down to steady my rifle and began looking for targets of opportunity.

As Charlie started over the hill toward us I had my weapon on full auto and got lucky taking out three or four right away. And they fell backward knocking down some that were coming up. After the initial burst I went to single shot to conserve ammo, aiming for head and chest.

The squad also started picking them off with two or three shots apiece as they would fall back on to their mates trying to climb the hill. This strategy went on for about twenty minutes and since we had the superior fire power and a better position we won the battle; however, the firefight had been fierce and frantic. I know when it started I had two 30-round magazines taped on my M-16 and twelve more in my vest. After the fire fight ended I only had one magazine left.

I believe we survived mainly because they apparently didn't have any decent communication to organize and started their ambush minutes too soon.

When the shooting tapered off and the squad leader rose and yelled for the squad to move out, Wergen became aware of something warm and sticky on his back. Thinking it was his blood, he didn't dare move for fear of making any wound worse. So Wergen asked one of the other guys how bad he was hit as he slowly bent forward. The guy smiled and told Wergen to relax and turn around. Wergen did and saw the tree he was next to, was nothing now but a tattered stump rising only about four inches above his head. The sticky goo was only sap from the tree. Wergen shook his head in relief, stood and joined the squad. They made their way to the landing zone and were picked up without further incident.

Wergen comments: This is the one battle I live over and over throughout my life. Maybe it's because it was my last fire fight...maybe it's because I thought I had been shot and was close to death...I dunno...maybe it's because I only had one magazine left.

But when the nightmares come...I'm running out of ammunition and they just keep coming and coming over the hill and I keep shooting, but they keep coming...and the nightmare never ends until I wake up screaming....it still happens to this day.

****

Wergen dubbed that battle the "tree sap mission," which would be his last, he vowed. *Dammit, his last—* he was going home in twenty-two days—alive!

Wergen comments: Anything I could do for the next three weeks to lessen my chance of being in harm's way, I did. I don't mean I would shirk duty and hide away or anything serious like that. But now I had some control over my destiny here. And my superior S-2 officer was also short. So he understood and didn't really interfere. After all he felt the same way.

Wergen next helped to develop and train a new *Rat* leader, which relieved him of doing any actual war-tunnel work in the jungle. All the old rats on his team were gone, so there was no difficulty in that move. He remained active in that non-combat tunnel rat role while training the new rat recruits in Di-An until the end of his tour.

Wergen comments: This short-timer duty basically kept me one step ahead of whoever was looking for me. It was actually pretty easy for me to be "invisible" until that day of separation. I believe my superiors understood and didn't push it. They all knew I had served my war duty.

****

On October 10, 1968 Staff Sergeant Thomas E. Wergen said good bye to everyone he knew at Di-An, grabbed his gear and enjoyed a 3-gun jeep escort to Bien Hoa airport. After formally transferring command to his replacement he carried his personal gear, souvenirs—consisting of a Russian Tokarev pistol and two Vietnamese grenades—and quickly boarded the plane to start him on his journey home.

Wergen comments: This was a very critical and dangerous period in leaving the country. You'd wait by the runway and suddenly a Boeing 707 would appear out of nowhere, perform a short-landing and quickly load 165 troops to take off as soon as possible. Of course they were trying to avoid catching a mortar or a rocket.

They'd land with minimum fuel so they could take off faster and then head for Hokkaido Air Base in Japan to catch a full load of fuel and then head to Guam for a second refueling and finally home to Oakland, California Army Base.

On my trip we were very fortunate to have about a 60-knot tail wind and did not need to stop in Guam – we all had fun yelling out a vote to go straight home when the pilot jokingly asked.

Their plane landed at Travis Air Force Base and they were all bussed to Oakland Air base. Somewhat settled, they were run through the de-lousing showers; given a new class A uniform, a steak dinner and their back pay before finally being set free. Wergen was now a civilian.

Wergen comments: In less than 24 hours I went from being a Viet Nam combat soldier to being a sunny California citizen. I hired a cab to take me to San Francisco International, bought a first class ticket to Los Angeles and stopped by an airport bar to get an ice tea glass full of VO.

I was unnerving fast. When I tried to board the plane the stewardess said I couldn't get on with a drink and I said "nicely" if she didn't get out of my way I would do as I promised my troops and bite the first round eye I saw "on the ass." She laughed, let me by and then gave me some ice and a cigar. Of course, it was a different world of flying back then.

When I landed at LAX it was strange: as I walked around I noticed no one would make eye contact with me. This also happened in my home town of Rosemead. Here I am walking down the street in dress greens, covered with medals and no one would even look at me. I know the world was at odds with the war...but here I am back from fighting for my country and they wouldn't acknowledge me. I was angry and confused.

When I walked up the driveway to my home I noticed all of the cars and it felt strange when I walked in the back door to see all my brothers and sisters standing there. My Mother asked what I wanted first. I told her anything green or white, as I basically had not seen fresh dairy or produce in over fifteen months. That was the beginning of my civilian rehabbing.

People say I was lucky after sixteen months of fighting in Vietnam. A kid of 21 was home – and still just a kid who was all in one piece, they said. I look at it as one man's adventure from childhood to manhood, albeit with a few gremlins thrown in. Just an average guy put into some very special circumstances…very hellish circumstances, I guess. But I made it through. Onward…

Epilogue
The Elite Tunnel Rats

Staff Sergeant Thomas Wergen's fifteen-month tour from July 1967 thru October 1968 was spent during Vietnam's bloodiest era in that war's history — including the infamous TET offensive — when most of the soldiers only wanted to serve their required time and rotate out before they became another grim statistic counting toward a government metal coffin. If not a statistic by the hands of the enemy, then perhaps by the hazardous elements of the God-awful jungle they had to survive in.

Wergen was not only bound by command but self-assurance to push himself beyond the normal and live out the perils of prowling those unfathomable conditions to search out and complete his missions of purging the enemy wherever, and in whatever way he could, while sometimes following his own self-made rules.

This included warfare deep into the abyss of jungle tunnels and above ground as well, while serving on secret Special Force missions of all types in enemy territory. Throughout the war and basically beginning in the spring of 1967, thousands of North Vietnamese tunnels were discovered by the allies. Wergen and his *Rats* inspected and destroyed close to 900 of them during his tour in Viet Nam.

During his harrowing period, Wergen had been shot, beat up, blown up twice and run over by a jeep, not to discount being bitten by enormous spiders and other venomous creatures. For his valor, he was awarded distinguishing honors. Besides the **Good Conduct Medal,** he received the **Bronze Star Medal** for meritorious service. And the citation he is most proud of, The **Combat Infantryman's Badge** awarded from the U.S. 5TH Special Forces Group (airborne), 1ST Special Forces. This honor is awarded to soldiers who actually engage in excess of thirty days of actual ground combat — some hand to hand.

Regardless of what element beat him down, whether it be the deep sadness of watching his best service friends die over there, or just the sheer stress of warfare, he was always eager to pick himself up, dust himself off, and move forward with his life — however long that might be. He knew if he didn't respond this way he'd be doomed to despondency. Of course, those elements remain with him.

In 1984 the Vietnam Veterans Memorial (The Wall), near the Lincoln Memorial in Washington D.C. was dedicated to the 2.7 million men and women in the U.S. military who served in the designated Viet Nam war zone. The names of over 58,000 casualties are etched into the granite.

Wergen comments: A few years ago I finally worked up the courage to go to the wall to visit my friends and high school classmates who were killed while serving there. When I traced my hand across my best friend's name, Lawrence Stapleton, I bowed my head and cried like a baby. Like most veterans I had brought home lots of demons, but this experience chased a lot of them away. I felt better.

Soft spoken and reticent, Wergen now lives a quiet retired life in Arizona. He listens to classical music while recounting his raw and exciting Vietnam War experiences, often demonstrating his expressive laugh and spirited sense of humor he never lost during the most traumatic and trying time of his life; however, he often lives through some rough moments when he recounts some of the war incidents, which at the time were part of his routine military maneuvers, but now appear ruthless.

Yet the honor that seems to continuously seep through Wergen's rugged demeanor centers on one fact: when the military powers needed someone to perform the seemingly impossible task in the deadly Vietnamese jungles they often called on him and his fearless pack of "Tunnel Rats" to see it through. And Sergeant Wergen is still quite pleased to remember that they nearly always succeeded.

I am quite proud to have told his story.

Riley St. James

Made in the USA
San Bernardino, CA
12 April 2019